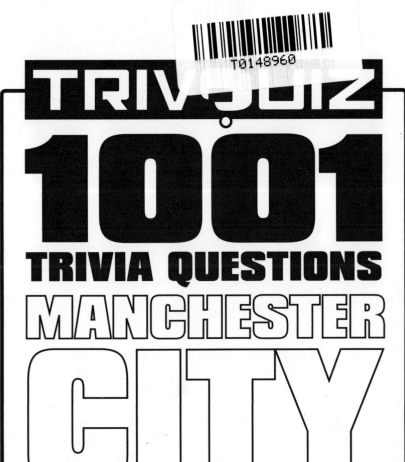

# TRIVQUIZ
# 1001
# TRIVIA QUESTIONS
# MANCHESTER
# CITY

FASCINATING FACTS! TRIVIA BRAINTEASERS!
WRITTEN AND ILLUSTRATED BY

DESIGNED BY JOE McGARRY

First published by Pitch Publishing, 2021

Pitch Publishing
A2 Yeoman Gate
Yeoman Way
Worthing
Sussex
BN13 3QZ
www.pitchpublishing.co.uk
info@pitchpublishing.co.uk

A CIP catalogue record is available for this book
from the British Library.

ISBN: 978 1 80150 017 3

Typesetting and origination by Pitch Publishing
Printed and bound in India by Replika Press Pvt. Ltd.

# 1001 TRIVIA QUESTIONS: MANCHESTER CITY

Other books in this series:

**1001 TRIVIA QUESTIONS: ARSENAL**
**1001 TRIVIA QUESTIONS: MANCHESTER UNITED**
**1001 TRIVIA QUESTIONS: NEWCASTLE UNITED**
**1001 TRIVIA QUESTIONS: TOTTENHAM HOTSPUR**
**1001 TRIVIA QUESTIONS: WEST HAM UNITED**
**1001 TRIVIA QUESTIONS: THIS DAY IN WORLD FOOTBALL**

## ACKNOWLEDGEMENTS

Thanks to Joe McGarry for his brilliant design work and his technical expertise. There would be no books without him!

Thanks to Debs McGarry for the research and art assistance.

Thanks to Luke McGarry for picking up the slack on the other features while we worked on this.

Thanks to all three for their patience!

Additional thanks to Tom and Andy at "Shoot! The Breeze" podcast and Rob Stokes for the additional research and scans!

## ABOUT STEVE McGARRY

A former record sleeve designer, whose clients included Joy Division, Steve McGarry is one of the most prolific and widely-published cartoonists and illustrators that Britain has ever produced. In the UK alone, his national newspaper daily strips include "Badlands", which ran for a dozen years in The Sun, "The Diary of Rock & Pop" in the Daily Star, "Pop Culture" in Today and "World Soccer Diary" in The Sun.

Over his four-decade career he has regularly graced the pages of soccer magazines Match, Match of the Day and Shoot! and his comics work ranges from Romeo in the 1970s and Look-In, Tiger and Oink! in the 1980s, SI for Kids and FHM in the 1990s, through to the likes of Viz, MAD and Toxic! When The People launched his Steve McGarry's 20th Century Heroes series, they billed him as the world's top cartoonist.

His sports features have been published worldwide since 1982 and he currently has two features – "Biographic" and "Kid Town" – in newspaper syndication, with a client list that includes the New York Daily News and The Washington Post.

In recent years, he has also created story art for such movies as "Despicable Me 2", "The Minions" and "The Secret Life of Pets".

Although Manchester born and bred, Steve has been based in California since 1989. A two-term former President of the National Cartoonists Society, his honours include Illustrator of the Year awards from the NCS and the Australian Cartoonists Association, and he is a recipient of the prestigious Silver T-Square for "outstanding service to the profession of cartooning". In 2013, he was elected President of the NCS Foundation, the charitable arm of the National Cartoonists Society. He is also the founder and director of US comics festival NCSFest.

# 1001 QUESTIONS

# "THE WELSH WIZARD"

FOUNDED BY CHURCH WARDENS AS **ST MARK'S (WEST GORTON)** IN 1880, THE AIM WAS TO PROVIDE AN OUTLET FOR YOUNG MEN IN AN AREA WHERE UNEMPLOYMENT WAS HIGH AND ALCOHOLISM AND GANG VIOLENCE PREVALENT. BY 1887, THE TEAM HAD MORPHED INTO **ARDWICK A.F.C.** -- BUT WHEN THE CLUB RAN INTO FINANCIAL PROBLEMS, IT WAS REFORMED IN 1894 AS **MANCHESTER CITY**. THE TEAM'S FIRST BIG STAR WAS TEENAGER **BILLY MEREDITH**, A MINER WHO CONTINUED TO WORK DOWN THE PIT IN HIS FIRST COUPLE OF YEARS WITH THE CLUB.

**1** NICKNAMED "*THE WELSH WIZARD*", *BILLY MEREDITH* CAPTAINED *CITY* IN THE 1904 FA CUP FINAL. HE SCORED THE ONLY GOAL OF THE GAME TO GIVE THE CLUB ITS FIRST MAJOR HONOUR. WHO WERE THE OPPONENTS THAT DAY?

**2** NAME THE VENUE FOR THAT 1904 FA CUP FINAL:
A) WEMBLEY    B) THE OVAL    C) CRYSTAL PALACE

**3** DURING GAMES, IT WAS *MEREDITH'S* HABIT TO:
A) SMOKE A CIGARETTE
B) SMOKE A PIPE
C) CHEW A TOOTHPICK

**4** AFTER HE WAS SUSPENDED WHEN *CITY* BECAME EMBROILED IN BRIBERY AND ILLEGAL PAYMENTS SCANDALS, HE SIGNED FOR WHICH TEAM IN 1906?

**5** HE RETURNED TO *CITY* IN 1921, AT THE AGE OF 47, AND WENT ON TO PLAY IN THE CLUB'S FINAL HOME GAME AT WHICH GROUND?

**6** *MEREDITH* PLAYED HIS FINAL GAME FOR *CITY* AT THE AGE OF 49 YEARS AND 245 DAYS. WHO BECAME THE CLUB'S YOUNGEST PLAYER, AGED 15 YEARS AND 314 DAYS ON HIS DEBUT IN 1962?

**7** NAME THREE OF THE FOUR PLAYERS WHO SCORED MORE THAN *MEREDITH'S* TOTAL OF 151 GOALS FOR THE CLUB.

**8** *MEREDITH* WAS TWICE A WINNER WITH *WALES* OF WHICH COMPETITION, THE OLDEST IN ASSOCIATION FOOTBALL?

**9** *MEREDITH* WON THE LAST OF HIS 48 INTERNATIONAL CAPS AT THE AGE OF 45 YEARS AND 229 DAYS, WHICH MAKES HIM THE OLDEST PLAYER TO REPRESENT *WALES*. WHICH *CITY* PLAYER, CAPTAIN OF THE TEAM THAT WON THE FA CUP IN 1956, EARNED HIS FINAL *WALES* CAP THAT YEAR AT THE AGE OF 35 YEARS AND 358 DAYS?

**10** WHICH SUBSEQUENT *MANCHESTER CITY* MANAGER, WHO WON HIS FINAL CAP FOR *WALES* IN 1999, AGED 35 YEARS AND 220 DAYS, WAS INDUCTED INTO THE ENGLISH FOOTBALL HALL OF FAME IN 2007, THE SAME YEAR AS *BILLY MEREDITH?*

# "WE'VE GOT GUARDIOLA!"

BORN IN SANTPEDOR ON JANUARY 18, 1971, *JOSEP "PEP" GUARDIOLA SALA* ENTERED *BARCELONA'S* FAMED *"LA MASIA"* ACADEMY AT THE AGE OF 13. *JOHAN CRUYFF* WAS BARELY A WEEK INTO THE *"BLAUGRANA"* MANAGER'S JOB WHEN HE SPOTTED THE SKINNY TEEN AND IMMEDIATELY CONVERTED HIM FROM A RIGHT-SIDED MIDFIELDER TO A PIVOT. *PEP* BECAME ONE OF THE WORLD'S BEST DEEP-LYING PLAYMAKERS ... AND SUBSEQUENTLY, ONE OF THE GREATEST COACHES THE GAME HAS EVER SEEN. IN HIS FIRST SEASON AS *BARCELONA* MANAGER, HE WON A SPANISH LEAGUE, CUP AND UEFA CHAMPIONS LEAGUE TREBLE!

**1** HOW MANY LA LIGA TITLES DID *PEP GUARDIOLA* WIN AS A *BARCELONA* PLAYER?

**2** *PEP* WAS A MEMBER OF THE 1992 EUROPEAN CUP-WINNING SIDE, *BARCELONA* BEATING *SAMPDORIA* 1-0 IN THE FINAL -- WHICH SUBSEQUENT *BARÇA* MANAGER SCORED THE WINNING GOAL?

**3** NAME TWO MANAGERS, BESIDES *CRUYFF*, UNDER WHOM *GUARDIOLA* PLAYED AT *BARCELONA*.

**4** NAME THE TWO ITALIAN TEAMS THAT *PEP* PLAYED FOR.

**5** HE SPENT TWO SEASONS PLAYING FOR *AL-AHLI SC* -- IN WHICH COUNTRY IS THAT TEAM BASED?

**6**   *PEP* WON AN OLYMPIC GOLD MEDAL WITH *SPAIN* IN WHICH YEAR?

**7**   HE REPLACED WHICH UEFA CHAMPIONS LEAGUE AND TWO-TIME LA LIGA WINNER AS COACH OF *BARCELONA* IN 2008?

**8**   HOW MANY TIMES DID *GUARDIOLA* WIN THE UEFA CHAMPIONS LEAGUE AS *BARCELONA* MANAGER?

**9**   *PEP* SUCCEEDED WHICH *BAYERN MUNICH* COACH WITHIN WEEKS OF THAT MANAGER WINNING THE TREBLE OF LEAGUE, CUP AND UEFA CHAMPIONS LEAGUE IN 2013?

**10**   *GUARDIOLA* RECRUITED *JUAN MANUEL LILLO* TO REPLACE THE DEPARTING ASSISTANT COACH *MIKEL ARTETA*. AT WHICH MEXICAN CLUB HAD *PEP* PLAYED UNDER *LILLO*?

# THE MIGHTY OAKES

BORN IN WINSFORD, CHESHIRE, ON SEPTEMBER 7, 1942, **ALAN OAKES** GAVE AWAY A PENALTY ON HIS **MANCHESTER CITY** DEBUT AT THE AGE OF 17. FORTUNATELY, **BERT TRAUTMANN** SAVED IT AND **OAKES** WENT ON TO BECOME ONE OF THE GREATEST SERVANTS IN THE CLUB'S HISTORY, BREAKING **TRAUTMANN'S** APPEARANCE RECORD IN THE PROCESS. HAVING MOVED INTO MANAGEMENT FOLLOWING HIS DEPARTURE FROM THE CLUB, HE UNSUCCESSFULLY APPLIED FOR THE **CITY** MANAGER'S JOB IN 1983.

**1** WITH 680 APPEARANCES, **ALAN OAKES** HOLDS THE ALL-TIME **CITY** RECORD, AHEAD OF WHICH GOALKEEPER ON 603 APPEARANCES?

**2** BETWEEN 1959 AND 1976, **OAKES** PLAYED UNDER SEVEN **MANCHESTER CITY** MANAGERS - CAN YOU NAME THEM?

**3** **OAKES** PLAYED MUCH OF HIS CAREER IN THE SAME **CITY** TEAM AS HIS COUSIN - CAN YOU NAME THAT PLAYER?

**4** EXCLUDING FA CHARITY SHIELD VICTORIES, NAME THE FIVE MAJOR HONOURS THAT **OAKES** WON WITH **MANCHESTER CITY**.

**5** **ALAN OAKES** MADE 777 DOMESTIC LEAGUE APPEARANCES IN HIS 25 YEARS IN ENGLISH LEAGUE FOOTBALL. ONLY SEVEN PLAYERS HAVE BETTERED THAT RECORD - CAN YOU NAME THE **MANCHESTER CITY** PLAYER WHO BEAT **ALAN'S** ACHIEVEMENT?

**6** **ALAN'S** GOALKEEPER SON, **MICHAEL OAKES**, WAS CAPPED FIVE TIMES BY **ENGLAND** AT UNDER-21 LEVEL. CAN YOU NAME ONE OF THE FOUR PREMIER LEAGUE OR FOOTBALL LEAGUE CLUBS FOR WHOM **MICHAEL** PLAYED?

**7** **OAKES** WAS TWICE AN FA CHARITY SHIELD WINNER WITH **CITY**, IN 1968 AND 1972. CAN YOU NAME THE TWO OPPOSING TEAMS?

**8** AFTER LEAVING **MANCHESTER CITY**, **ALAN** SPENT SIX YEARS AS PLAYER-MANAGER AT WHICH CLUB, NOTABLY LAUNCHING THE CAREER OF **IAN RUSH** DURING HIS TENURE?

**9**    **ALAN** MADE ONE APPEARANCE FOR WHICH NON-LEAGUE CHESHIRE CLUB, WHOSE NICKNAME IS **"THE TRICKIES"?**

**10**    **ALAN'S** FINAL GAME CAME AT THE AGE OF 41 YEARS AND 60 DAYS OLD WHEN HE APPEARED FOR WHICH TEAM, NICKNAMED **"THE VALIANTS"**, AT THE CLUB'S **VALE PARK** GROUND?

# VIVA ESPAÑA

BORN IN GRAN CANARIA ON JANUARY 8, 1986, **DAVID SILVA** LAUNCHED HIS CAREER WITH **VALENCIA**, JOINING **CITY** IN 2010. IN HIS TEN SEASONS WITH THE CLUB HE WON FOUR PREMIER LEAGUES, TWO FA CUPS AND FIVE LEAGUE CUPS. A WORLD CUP AND TWO-TIME EUROPEAN CHAMPIONSHIP WINNER WITH **SPAIN**, HE JOINED **REAL SOCIEDAD** IN 2020 AND WON THE COPA DEL REY IN HIS DEBUT SEASON.

NAME THE FOLLOWING SPANISH **MANCHESTER CITY** PLAYERS:

**1**  2010 WORLD CUP AND 2012 EUROPEAN CHAMPIONSHIP WINNER WITH **SPAIN** WHO WON EUROPA LEAGUE TITLES WITH **SEVILLA** EITHER SIDE OF HIS FOUR SEASONS WITH **CITY**.

**2**  FORMER **REAL MADRID** AND **OSASUNA** DEFENSIVE MIDFIELDER, A LEAGUE CHAMPION WITH **BENFICA**, HE WON A PREMIER LEAGUE AND LEAGUE CUP WITH **PELLEGRINI'S CITY** BEFORE WINNING THE LEAGUE WITH **ZENIT SAINT PETERSBURG**.

**3**  SPANISH DEFENDER, SIGNED BY **SVEN-GÖRAN ERIKSSON**, PLAYED INFREQUENTLY UNDER **HUGHES** AND **MANCINI** AND WENT ON TO PLAY FOR **NORWICH CITY**, **LAZIO** AND **LAS PALMAS**.

**4**  NICKNAMED **"THE BEAST OF VALLECAS"**, HE SCORED 23 GOALS IN 2013-14, HIS DEBUT SEASON FOR **CITY**, DESPITE NOT SCORING FROM JANUARY ONWARDS! SUBSEQUENT TEAMS RANGED FROM **VALENCIA** AND **BEŞIKTAŞ** TO **MIDDLESBROUGH** AND **AL-NASR**.

**5**  SIGNED FROM **VALENCIA**, HE INHERITED **SILVA'S** NUMBER 21 SHIRT.

**6**  LEFT BACK LOANED OUT TO **NEW YORK CITY**, **GIRONA**, **MALLORCA** AND **NAC BREDA** BEFORE JOINING **PSV EINDHOVEN**, RETURNING TO **CITY** AND THEN SIGNING FOR **RB LEIPZIG**.

**7**  FRENCH-BORN DEFENDER WHO SWITCHED ALLEGIANCE TO **SPAIN** AND WAS IMMEDIATELY CALLED UP FOR THE UEFA EURO 2020 SQUAD.

**8**  A CLUB RECORD £62.6 MILLION SIGNING FROM **ATLÉTICO MADRID**, HE SCORED THE WINNING GOAL IN THE 2020 LEAGUE CUP FINAL.

**9**  A GRADUATE OF LA MASIA, HE RETURNED TO **BARCELONA** IN 2021 ON A FREE TRANSFER AS A PREMIER LEAGUE WINNER.

**10**  FRUSTRATED WITH A LACK OF FIRST TEAM OPPORTUNITIES, HE PUSHED FOR HIS 2019 MOVE TO **REAL MADRID** AND SUBSEQUENTLY IMPRESSED ON LOAN WITH **AC MILAN**.

# OFF TO THE TOFFEES!

THE PROLIFIC **TOMMY JOHNSON**, A FORMER SHIPYARD APPRENTICE WHO WENT ON TO PLAY FOR **ENGLAND**, HIT A CLUB RECORD 38 GOALS FOR **CITY** IN THE 1928-29 SEASON. WHEN "**TOSH**" WAS SOLD TO **EVERTON** IN 1930, FANS WERE SO INCENSED THAT ATTENDANCE NUMBERS DROPPED BY 7,000! HE WON A LEAGUE TITLE WITH **"THE TOFFEES"** AND PLAYED IN THE TEAM THAT DEFEATED **CITY** IN THE 1933 FA CUP FINAL.

IDENTIFY THESE **CITY** PLAYERS WHO LATER PLAYED FOR **EVERTON**:

**1** CLUB STALWART AND CAPTAIN WHO LED **CITY** OUT AT WEMBLEY THREE TIMES WITHOUT SUCCESS, HE ENDED HIS PLAYING CAREER AS A 1987 LEAGUE CHAMPION WITH **EVERTON**.

**2** FORMER **LEEDS UNITED** AND **ASTON VILLA** FAVOURITE, A VERSATILE MIDFIELDER WHO WON TWO LEAGUE TITLES WITH **CITY** BEFORE JOINING **EVERTON** IN 2019.

**3** A EUROPEAN CUP WINNER IN HIS TEENS, HE PLAYED FOR **EVERTON** AND **BOLTON WANDERERS** AFTER LEAVING **CITY**, FINISHED HIS PLAYING DAYS IN THE STATES, THEN MANAGED AND COACHED EXTENSIVELY BEFORE JOINING **CITY'S** COACHING STAFF IN 2009.

**4** **CITY** LEFT-BACK WHO WAS SOLD TO **EVERTON** BY **HOWARD KENDALL** IN 1990. IN EIGHT YEARS AT GOODISON PARK HE WON THE FA CUP IN 1995, BUT WAS SOLD TO **SHEFFIELD WEDNESDAY** AFTER **KENDALL** WAS APPOINTED **EVERTON** BOSS IN 1997.

**5** FRENCH CENTRAL DEFENDER WHO WON THE 2008 FA CUP WITH **PORTSMOUTH** AFTER LEAVING **CITY**, BEFORE SPENDING SIX SEASONS WITH **EVERTON** AND ENDING HIS CAREER AT **BOURNEMOUTH**.

**6** JOURNEYMAN GOALKEEPER WHO WAS FREQUENTLY ROTATED WITH **NICKY WEAVER** DURING K**EVIN KEEGAN'S** TENURE AT **CITY**, HE WON PROMOTIONS WITH **CITY**, **CRYSTAL PALACE** AND **STOKE CITY**, SPENT THREE YEARS WITH **STOCKPORT COUNTY**, TWO YEARS WITH **PRESTON NORTH END** AND WAS APPOINTED **SALFORD CITY** GOALKEEPING COACH IN 2018.

**7** NICKNAMED *"BERTIE BASSETT"* BY *EVERTON* FANS BECAUSE HE PLAYED IN *"ALLSORTS OF POSITIONS"*, HE WON THE LEAGUE AND UEFA CUP WINNERS' CUP IN 1985 WITH THE CLUB, PLAYED FOR *SHEFFIELD WEDNESDAY* AND *CITY*, RETURNED TO *EVERTON* IN 1991 AND LATER PLAYED FOR *LUTON TOWN, BURNLEY* AND *CARDIFF CITY.*

**8** FA CUP WINNING DEFENDER WITH *WIMBLEDON*, HE JOINED *CITY* IN 1992, PLAYED FOR THE *REPUBLIC OF IRELAND* AT THE 1994 WORLD CUP, PLAYED FOR *CHELSEA* AND *EVERTON*, WAS A FIRST DIVISION CHAMPION WITH *FULHAM* AND THEN PLAYED IN THE STATES AND NEW ZEALAND.

**9** WINGER WHO WAS A REGULAR AT *CITY* AFTER SIGNING FROM *WEST HAM UNITED*, HE JOINED *HOWARD KENDALL'S EVERTON* IN 1991, PLAYED FOR A LENGTHY LIST OF CLUBS, BUT WAS JAILED IN 2005 ON DRUGS TRAFFICKING CHARGES.

**10** CAPPED 53 TIMES BY *ENGLAND*, HE WAS A CLUB LEGEND AT *ASTON VILLA*, WON A PREMIER LEAGUE AND FA CUP WITH *CITY*, PLAYED FOUR SEASONS AT *EVERTON* AND JOINED *WEST BROMWICH ALBION* IN 2017.

# NOT FROM ROUND HERE

THE FIRST GEORGIAN TO PLAY FOR *CITY*, *GEORGI KINKLADZE'S* DEBUT SEASON AT THE CLUB ENDED IN RELEGATION FROM THE PREMIER LEAGUE. SKILFUL AND WILDLY INVENTIVE, HE WAS BELOVED BY *CITY* FANS ... BUT NOT SO MUCH BY *FRANK CLARK'S* REPLACEMENT *JOE ROYLE*, WHO CONSIDERED THE PLAYMAKER A LUXURY THAT A RELEGATION-BATTLING TEAM COULD NOT AFFORD. HE WAS MOVED ON TO *AJAX*, ALTHOUGH HE LATER RETURNED TO ENGLAND WITH *DERBY COUNTY*.

**1** *GELSON FERNANDES* AND *GIUSEPPE MAZZARELLI* BOTH PLAYED INTERNATIONAL FOOTBALL FOR WHICH COUNTRY?

**2** NAME *CITY'S* ONLY *ZIMBABWE* INTERNATIONAL, A STRIKER WHO PLIED HIS TRADE WITH *AUXERRE, PORTSMOUTH, SUNDERLAND* AND *BLACKBURN ROVERS*.

**3** *MANCHESTER CITY* LEGEND *SHAUN GOATER* SCORED 32 GOALS IN HIS 36 APPEARANCES FOR WHICH COUNTRY?

**4** WHICH *CITY* PLAYER MADE 103 APPEARANCES FOR *CROATIA* AND WAS ON THE LOSING SIDE IN THE 2018 WORLD CUP FINAL?

**5** NAME THE *MANCHESTER CITY* PLAYER WHO REPRESENTED *CHINA* AT THE 2002 WORLD CUP.

**6** STRIKER *VALERI BOJINOV* WAS ONE OF TWO *BULGARIA* INTERNATIONALS SIGNED TO *CITY* IN 2007 -- WHO WAS THE OTHER?

**7** WHO BECAME *CITY'S* FIRST UKRAINIAN PLAYER WHEN HE SIGNED IN 2016?

**8** NAME ONE OF THE TWO *MONTENEGRO* INTERNATIONALS WHO HAVE PLAYED FOR *CITY*.

**9** **COSTEL PANTILIMON**, THE GIANT GOALKEEPER WHOSE CAREER HAS INCLUDED SPELLS AT **CITY, SUNDERLAND, WATFORD** AND **NOTTINGHAM FOREST,** IS A NATIVE OF WHICH COUNTRY?

**10** NAME THE FIRST **POLAND** INTERNATIONAL TO EVER PLAY FOR **CITY,** WHOSE SEVEN GOALS IN THE LAST EIGHT GAMES OF THE SEASON HELPED THE CLUB STAVE OFF RELEGATION IN 1979. HE WAS KILLED IN A CAR CRASH IN CALIFORNIA IN 1989.

# THE PLUMBER AND "THE POTTERS"

EVEN AFTER TURNING PROFESSIONAL WITH *CITY* IN 1960, *HARRY DOWD* CONTINUED WORKING FOR SOME TIME AS A PLUMBER. A MEMBER OF THE TEAM THAT WON THE 1969 FA CUP, HE SPENT SOME OF HIS FINAL SEASON WITH *CITY* ON LOAN AT *STOKE CITY* AS BACK-UP TO *GORDON BANKS*, BEFORE MOVING ON TO *OLDHAM ATHLETIC* IN 1970.

IDENTIFY THESE *CITY* PLAYERS WHO WENT ON TO PLAY FOR *STOKE CITY*:

**1** *IVORY COAST* STRIKER, PREVIOUSLY A GOALSCORING SENSATION AT *SWANSEA CITY*, WAS LOANED OUT TO *STOKE CITY* IN 2016 WHEN HIS *CITY* CAREER FAILED TO CATCH FIRE.

**2** SIGNED FROM *BLACKBURN ROVERS* IN 1961 AS A REPLACEMENT WHEN *DENIS LAW* LEFT FOR *TORINO*, HE WAS *CITY'S* TOP SCORER IN HIS DEBUT SEASON BUT RELEGATION IN HIS SECOND PROMPTED HS SALE TO *"THE POTTERS"*.

**3** *REPUBLIC OF IRELAND* MIDFIELDER NICKNAMED *"SUPERMAN"* BY *CITY* FANS AFTER HE REVEALED HIS S*UPERMAN* UNDERWEAR IN A GOAL CELEBRATION!

**4** SON OF OLYMPIC GOLD MEDALLIST *ANN PACKER* AND 400M RUNNER *ROBBIE*, HE WAS A *CITY* REGULAR FOR 12 SEASONS AND LATER PLAYED FOR AND MANAGED BOTH *PORT VALE* AND *MACCLESFIELD TOWN*.

**5** *ASTON VILLA* AND *ENGLAND* RIGHT-BACK WHO PLAYED FOR *EVERTON* AND *MANCHESTER UNITED* BEFORE SPENDING TWO SEASONS AT *CITY*, THEN JOINED *STOKE CITY* IN 1988.

**6** BEGAN HIS CAREER AT *STOKE*, WON TWO LEAGUE TITLES AND THE UEFA CUP WINNERS' CUP WITH *EVERTON*, SPENT TIME WITH *ESPANYOL* AND *ASTON VILLA* BEFORE JOINING *CITY*, BRIEFLY REJOINED *STOKE* IN 1992, BEFORE TWO SPELLS AT *BURNLEY* INTERRUPTED BY A SEASON WITH *SHEFFIELD UNITED*.

**7** **SWEDEN** INTERNATIONAL STRIKER, THE MAJORITY OF HIS SEVEN YEARS WITH **CITY** WERE SPENT ON LOAN AT **BROMMAPOJKARNA, BURNLEY, FEYENOORD, STOKE CITY** AND **CELTIC,** BEFORE HE SIGNED FOR **CELTA** IN 2015.

**8** **ENGLAND** REGULAR VOTED **CITY** PLAYER OF THE YEAR THREE TIMES IN HIS LENGTHY MAINE ROAD CAREER, HE LATER KEPT GOAL FOR **BRIGHTON & HOVE ALBION, NORWICH CITY** AND **STOKE** FOLLOWING A SPELL IN THE STATES.

**9** **CITY** LEGEND WHO WON EVERY DOMESTIC HONOUR AND THE UEFA CUP WINNERS' CUP WITH THE CLUB BEFORE HELPING **STOKE** GAIN PROMOTION TO THE TOP FLIGHT IN 1979, LATER MOVING ON TO **BOLTON WANDERERS** AND **ROCHDALE.**

**10** HAVING SIGNED FOR **CITY** FROM BLACKPOOL IN 1987, HE WON THE FA CUP WITH **TOTTENHAM HOTSPUR,** SPENT SPELLS ON LOAN WITH FOUR DIFFERENT ENGLISH CLUBS WHILE A **LIVERPOOL** PLAYER, SIGNED FOR **SUNDERLAND** AND **STOKE** AND THEN ENDED HIS PLAYING DAYS AT **WORKINGTON.**

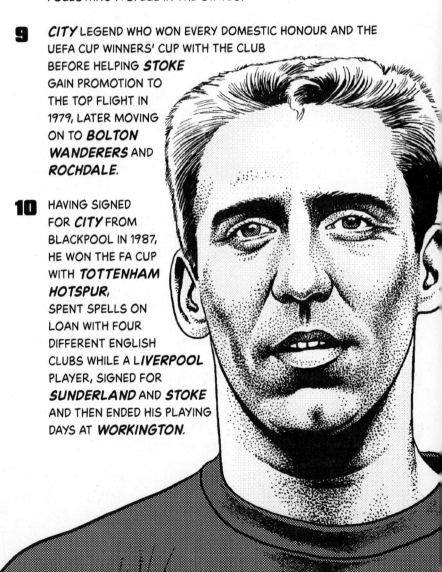

# "THE BOSNIAN DIAMOND"

**EDIN DŽEKO** JOINED **CITY** IN JANUARY, 2011, AND WON THE FA CUP THAT SEASON. THE NEXT TERM, HE HELPED FIRE THE CLUB TO A FIRST LEAGUE TITLE IN 44 YEARS. **"THE BOSNIAN DIAMOND"** SUBSEQUENTLY ADDED A LEAGUE CUP AND SECOND PREMIER LEAGUE TITLE TO HIS TALLY.

**1** **EDIN** WON A BUNDESLIGA TITLE WITH WHICH CLUB?

**2** HIS £27 MILLION TRANSFER TO **CITY** WAS THE SECOND-HIGHEST FEE PAID BY THE CLUB TO THAT POINT FOLLOWING THE TRANSFER OF WHICH **REAL MADRID** PLAYER IN 2008?

**3** HIS FIRST MEDAL WITH **CITY** CAME WITH THE 2011 FA CUP FINAL VICTORY OVER WHICH TEAM?

**4** HE BECAME THE FIRST **CITY** PLAYER TO SCORE FOUR GOALS IN A PREMIER LEAGUE GAME IN THE 5-1 WIN OVER WHICH TEAM IN 2011?

**5** **SERGIO AGÜERO** FAMOUSLY SCORED THE LAST-GASP WINNER THAT GAVE CITY A 3-2 WIN OVER **QUEENS PARK RANGERS** TO CLAIM THE 2012 PREMIER LEAGUE TITLE, AFTER **DŽEKO** HAD SCORED AN EQUALISER IN EXTRA-TIME -- BUT WHO OPENED THE SCORING FOR CITY THAT DAY?

**6** HE WON A LEAGUE CUP MEDAL IN THE 2014 WIN OVER WHICH TEAM?

**7** **DŽEKO** JOINED WHICH ITALIAN TEAM IN 2015?

**8** NAME HIS ERSTWHILE **MANCHESTER CITY** TEAMMATE WHO, IN 2017, JOINED THE SAME ITALIAN TEAM AS **DŽEKO**.

**9** IN ITALY, HE PLAYED THE 2018/19 SEASON UNDER WHICH COACH WHO HAD PREVIOUSLY WON AN ENGLISH PREMIER LEAGUE TITLE?

**10** **BOSNIA AND HERZEGOVINA** APPEARED AT A WORLD CUP FOR THE FIRST TIME IN 2014. AGAINST WHICH COUNTRY DID **EDIN DŽEKO** SCORE IN A 3-1 VICTORY, HIS NATION'S FIRST EVER WORLD CUP WIN?

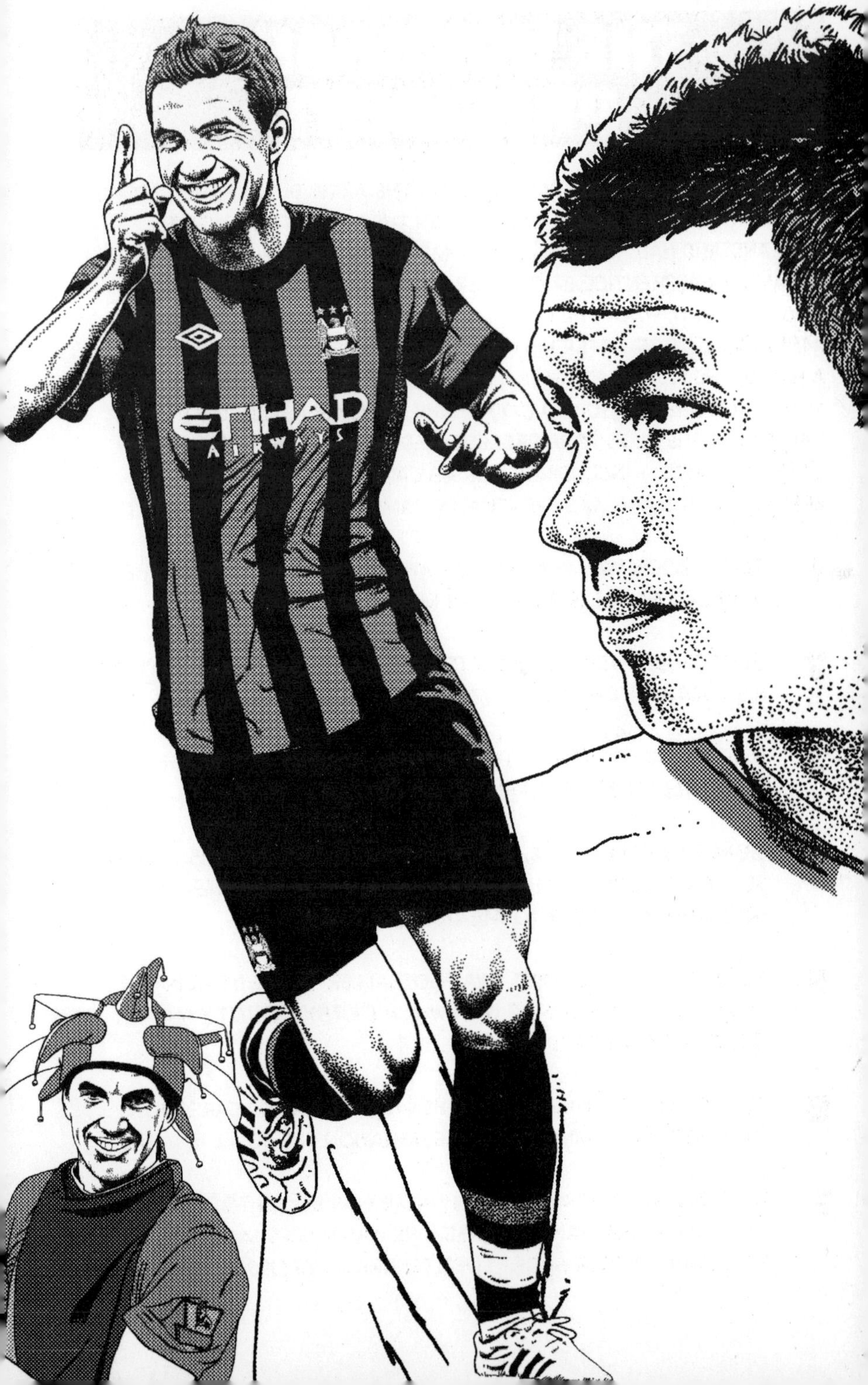
ETIHAD
AIRWAYS

# THE HONORARY PRESIDENT

RAISED IN INDIA WHILE HIS DAD SERVED IN THE ARMY DURING THE SECOND WORLD WAR, *TONY BOOK* WAS 12 WHEN THE FAMILY RETURNED TO ENGLAND AND HAD NEVER PLAYED COMPETITIVE FOOTBALL. AT 16, HE BECAME AN APPRENTICE BRICKLAYER, AND AT 18, WAS CONSCRIPTED INTO THE ARMY, WHERE HE PLAYED FOOTBALL FOR THE *ROYAL ARMY MEDICAL CORPS*. AFTER HIS NATIONAL SERVICE, WHILE WORKING AS A BRICKIE, HE PLAYED FOR NON-LEAGUE *FROME TOWN*. HE WAS 32 YEARS OLD WHEN HE JOINED *CITY* -- AND HE NEVER REALLY LEFT! AFTER CAPTAINING THE CLUB TO UNPRECEDENTED HEIGHTS, *"SKIP"* MANAGED *CITY* FIVE TIMES -- INCLUDING FOUR AS CARETAKER -- COACHED AT VARIOUS LEVELS AND WAS EVENTUALLY NAMED HONORARY PRESIDENT!

**1** *TONY BOOK* WAS PLAYING FOR WHICH NON-LEAGUE TEAM WHEN *MALCOLM ALLISON* BECAME MANAGER IN 1962?

**2** *BOOK* FOLLOWED *ALLISON* TO NORTH AMERICA IN 1963 TO PLAY HIS FOOTBALL IN WHICH CITY?

**3** *BOOK* FINALLY ENTERED THE FOOTBALL LEAGUE AT THE AGE OF 30 WHEN *ALLISON* SIGNED HIM TO WHICH CLUB IN 1964?

**4** SIGNED TO *CITY* IN 1966, *BOOK* WAS MADE CAPTAIN IN HIS SECOND SEASON FOLLOWING THE DEPARTURE OF WHICH *NORTHERN IRELAND* MIDFIELDER TO *MIDDLESBROUGH?*

**5** *BOOK* WAS NAMED JOINT FWA FOOTBALLER OF THE YEAR IN 1969, SHARING THE AWARD WITH WHICH *DERBY COUNTY* AND *SCOTLAND* MIDFIELDER?

**6** HE WAS STILL PLAYING IN 1973 WHEN HE WAS NAMED CARETAKER MANAGER FOLLOWING WHOSE RESIGNATION DUE TO ILL HEALTH?

**7** THE FOLLOWING YEAR, HAVING HUNG UP HIS BOOTS TO TAKE THE JOB OF ASSISTANT MANAGER, HE WAS NAMED MANAGER FOLLOWING WHOSE SHORT-LIVED TENURE AS *CITY* BOSS?

**8** WHAT WAS THE ONLY TROPHY *BOOK* WON AS *CITY* MANAGER?

**9** HE WAS BRIEFLY CHIEF SCOUT AT WHICH CLUB IN 1997 UNDER THE MANAGEMENT OF FORMER *CITY* BOSS *BRIAN HORTON?*

**10** *BOOK* LAST TOOK CHARGE OF *CITY* IN A CARETAKER CAPACITY FOR ONE GAME IN 1993, FOLLOWING WHICH MANAGER'S DISMISSAL?

# "EL APACHE" TEVEZ

RAISED IN AN AREA OF BUENOS AIRES SO ROUGH AND DANGEROUS THAT IT WAS NICKNAMED *"FORT APACHE"*, *CARLOS TEVEZ* WAS ACCIDENTALLY SCALDED WITH BOILING WATER WHEN HE WAS A TODDLER. THROUGHOUT HIS CAREER, THE TENACIOUS AND COMBATIVE FORWARD STEADFASTLY REFUSED PLASTIC SURGERY, INSISTING THAT THE SCARS HE BEARS ARE A REMINDER OF THE BATTLES HE FACED.

**1** *TEVEZ* BEGAN HIS CAREER WITH -- AND HAS SUBSEQUENTLY TWICE RETURNED TO -- WHICH BUENOS AIRES CLUB?

**2** HAVING WON NUMEROUS HONOURS IN ARGENTINA, HE JOINED WHICH BRAZILIAN TEAM IN 2005?

**3** *TEVEZ* WON THREE CONSECUTIVE SOUTH AMERICAN FOOTBALLER OF THE YEAR AWARDS. NAME ONE OF THE TWO OTHER PLAYERS WHO HAD PREVIOUSLY WON THE AWARD THREE TIMES.

**4** HE WON AN OLYMPIC GOLD MEDAL WITH *ARGENTINA* IN 2004, SCORING THE ONLY GOAL OF THE GAME TO DEFEAT WHICH NATION IN THE FINAL?

**5** HE MOVED TO ENGLISH FOOTBALL IN 2006 WHEN HE JOINED **WEST HAM UNITED** IN A DOUBLE DEAL THAT INCLUDED WHICH OTHER **ARGENTINA** INTERNATIONAL?

**6** HE WAS A PREMIER LEAGUE WINNER IN BOTH OF HIS SEASONS WITH **MANCHESTER UNITED**, AND WON A CHAMPIONS LEAGUE MEDAL WHEN **UNITED** DEFEATED WHICH TEAM IN THE 2008 FINAL?

**7** PLAYING FOR **CITY**, HE WON THE 2011 GOLDEN BOOT, SHARING THE AWARD WITH WHICH **MANCHESTER UNITED** PLAYER?

**8** HE SPENT MONTHS ON *"GARDENING LEAVE"* AFTER FALLING OUT WITH **CITY** MANAGER **ROBERTO MANCINI** AFTER APPARENTLY REFUSING TO WARM UP TO COME ON AS SUBSTITUTE IN A UEFA CHAMPIONS LEAGUE GAME AGAINST WHICH TEAM?

**9** **TEVEZ** WON TWO LEAGUE TITLES AND WAS NAMED SERIE A FOOTBALLER OF THE YEAR DURING HIS TWO SEASONS WITH WHICH ITALIAN CLUB?

**10** **TEVEZ** PLAYED FOR WHICH CHINESE SUPER LEAGUE TEAM?

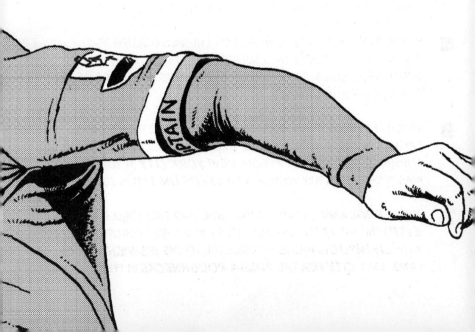

# "LIFE IS SO GOOD IN AMERICA ..."

AN FA CUP WINNER WITH *SUNDERLAND* AND A LEAGUE CUP WINNER WITH *CITY*, *ENGLAND* INTERNATIONAL *DENNIS TUEART* LEFT MAINE ROAD FOR GIANTS STADIUM AND *THE NEW YORK COSMOS* IN 1978. HE WON SOCCER BOWL '78 -- A GAME IN WHICH HE SCORED TWICE AND WAS NAMED MVP -- BEFORE RETURNING TO *CITY* IN 1980. HE LATER BECAME A *CITY* DIRECTOR BUT LEFT THE BOARD IN 2007.

**1** *UNITED STATES* INTERNATIONAL GOALKEEPER *ZACK STEFFEN* JOINED *CITY* FROM WHICH MLS TEAM?

**2** WHICH CENTRE-BACK LEFT THE *SEATTLE SOUNDERS* IN 1981 TO PLAY FOR HIS FATHER AT *MANCHESTER CITY?*

**3** WHICH SUBSEQUENT *CITY* MANAGER WAS PLAYER/MANAGER WITH THE *PHILADELPHIA FURY*, WON THE 1979 SOCCER BOWL WITH *VANCOUVER WHITECAPS*, AND SPENT TIME PLAYING OVERSEAS IN SOUTH AFRICA, AUSTRALIA AND HONG KONG?

**4** *POLAND* INTERNATIONAL *KAZIMIERZ DEYNA* LEFT *CITY* FOR CALIFORNIA IN 1981 TO PLAY FOR WHICH MLS TEAM?

**5** WHICH ERSTWHILE *CITY* STRIKER WON THE MLS GOLDEN BOOT TWICE, AND WON THREE MLS SUPPORTERS SHIELDS WITH *NEW YORK RED BULLS*, BEFORE PLAYING FOR *LOS ANGELES FC* AND THE *COLUMBUS CREW?*

**6** WHICH PLAYER, BORN IN STOKE ON TRENT, PLAYED HIGH SCHOOL SOCCER IN THE STATES, WAS THE #1 OVERALL PICK IN THE 2016 MLS SUPERDRAFT, JOINED *CITY* FROM *NEW YORK CITY* IN 2018 AND WAS A CHAMPIONSHIP WINNER WITH *LEEDS UNITED* IN 2020?

**7** WHICH *ENGLAND* INTERNATIONAL, WHO HAD TWO SPELLS WITH *EVERTON*, WON FOUR LEAGUE TITLES AND THREE EUROPEAN CUPS WITH *LIVERPOOL*, AND IS AN INDUCTEE TO THE *IPSWICH* HALL OF FAME, LEFT *CITY* FOR THE *TULSA ROUGHNECKS* IN 1984?

**8** WHICH STALWART OF THE *CITY* COACHING STAFF HAD SPELLS WITH *THE ATLANTA CHIEFS*, *THE FORT LAUDERDALE STRIKERS* AND *THE MINNESOTA STRIKERS* BEFORE BEGINNING HIS COACHING CAREER WITH *BARROW* IN 1984?

**9** NAME THE FORMER *CITY* PLAYER, WHO WON TWO LEAGUE TITLES AND THE UEFA CUP WINNERS' CUP WITH *EVERTON* AS A PLAYER, AND WHOSE MANAGEMENT POSTS INCLUDE *BURNLEY* AND *SHEFFIELD UNITED*, WHO WON MULTIPLE HONOURS AS HEAD COACH OF *ORLANDO CITY* BEFORE TAKING THE REINS AT *MINNESOTA UNITED*.

**10** WHICH *CITY ELITE DEVELOPMENT SQUAD* MANAGER ACCEPTED THE POST OF MANAGER OF *NEW YORK CITY FC* IN 2016?

# AUSTRALIAN, THAI AND INDIAN TAKEAWAYS

HAVING WON DOMESTIC AND UEFA CUP HONOURS WITH **LIVERPOOL**, **ROBBIE FOWLER'S** TRAVELS TOOK HIM TO **LEEDS UNITED**, **CITY**, BACK TO **LIVERPOOL** AND ON TO **CARDIFF CITY**. AFTER A THREE MONTH DALLIANCE WITH **BLACKBURN ROVERS**, HE CAST HIS NET WIDER, PLAYING IN AUSTRALIA WITH **NORTH QUEENSLAND FURY** AND **PERTH GLORY**, BEFORE LAUNCHING HIS MANAGEMENT CAREER IN THAILAND AS PLAYER/MANAGER WITH **MUANGTHONG UNITED**. HE FOLLOWED A SPELL AT THE HELM OF **BRISBANE ROAR** BY TAKING THE REINS AT INDIAN SUPER LEAGUE TEAM **EAST BENGAL** IN 2020.

**1** WHICH **EVERTON**, **ASTON VILLA**, **LIVERPOOL**, **CITY** AND **ENGLAND** MIDFIELDER, WHO MANAGED **SWINDON TOWN** AND **BLACKPOOL** TO PROMOTIONS, WAS **PERTH GLORY** MANAGER IN THE INAUGURAL AUSTRALIAN A-LEAGUE SEASON IN 2005?

**2** WHICH **AUSTRALIA** INTERNATIONAL COMBATIVE FIREBRAND BEGAN AND ENDED HIS CAREER IN HIS HOMELAND, PLAYED IN ITALY AND SWITZERLAND, SPENT SIX SEASONS WITH **CITY** FROM 1998 AND WAS PLAYER OF THE YEAR AT BOTH **CITY** AND **LEICESTER CITY?**

**3** WHICH **AUSTRALIA** INTERNATIONAL JOINED **CITY** FROM **MELBOURNE CITY** IN 2016 AND WAS LOANED TO **HUDDERSFIELD TOWN**, WITH WHOM HE GAINED PROMOTION TO THE TOP FLIGHT?

**4** NAME THE **REPUBLIC OF IRELAND** STRIKER WHO FOLLOWED HIS **ARSENAL**, **CITY** AND **SUNDERLAND** PLAYING DAYS WITH A BRIEF SPELL IN THAILAND WITH **BEC TERO SASANA?**

**5** IN 2012, WHICH FORMER **CITY** MANAGER WAS UNVEILED AS THE TECHNICAL DIRECTOR OF **BEC TERO SASANA**, FOLLOWING HIS DEPARTURE FROM **LEICESTER CITY** AND PRIOR TO BECOMING HEAD COACH OF **GUANGZHOU R&F** OF THE CHINESE SUPER LEAGUE?

**6** NAME THE FORMER THAILAND PRIME MINISTER WHO BOUGHT **MANCHESTER CITY** IN 2007 FOR £81.6 MILLION.

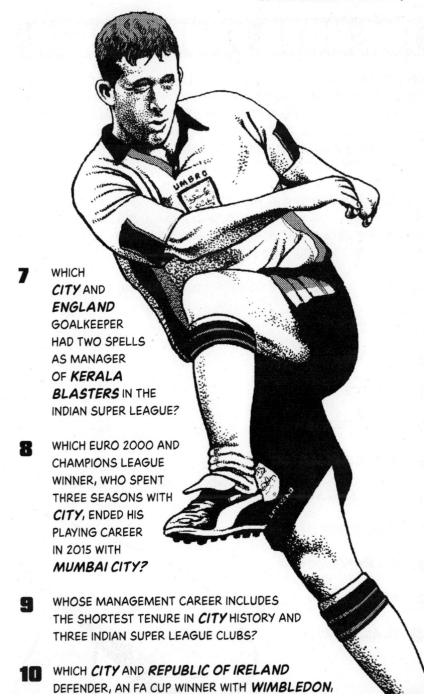

**7** WHICH *CITY* AND *ENGLAND* GOALKEEPER HAD TWO SPELLS AS MANAGER OF *KERALA BLASTERS* IN THE INDIAN SUPER LEAGUE?

**8** WHICH EURO 2000 AND CHAMPIONS LEAGUE WINNER, WHO SPENT THREE SEASONS WITH *CITY*, ENDED HIS PLAYING CAREER IN 2015 WITH *MUMBAI CITY?*

**9** WHOSE MANAGEMENT CAREER INCLUDES THE SHORTEST TENURE IN *CITY* HISTORY AND THREE INDIAN SUPER LEAGUE CLUBS?

**10** WHICH *CITY* AND *REPUBLIC OF IRELAND* DEFENDER, AN FA CUP WINNER WITH *WIMBLEDON*, COACHED *KERALA BLASTERS* AND *SOUTH UNITED?*

# THE BOYS FROM BRAZIL

**BRAZIL** STAR **ROBINHO** WAS ALL SET TO LEAVE **REAL MADRID** TO JOIN **LUIZ FELIPE SCOLARI'S CHELSEA** ... UNTIL THE SPANIARDS TOOK UMBRAGE UPON LEARNING THAT **ROBINHO** SHIRTS WERE ALREADY ON SALE IN THE **CHELSEA** SHOP! ON DEADLINE DAY OF THE 2008 TRANSFER WINDOW, **SHEIKH MANSOUR** AND THE **ABU DHABI UNITED GROUP** PURCHASED **CITY** AND IMMEDIATELY SWOOPED IN TO MAKE **ROBINHO** THE CLUB'S FIRST STATEMENT SIGNING. HOWEVER, THE DEAL ALMOST FELL THROUGH WHEN SOMEONE IN THE **CITY** OFFICE PUT THE CLUB'S OFFER IN THE FAX MACHINE THE WRONG WAY ROUND, AND ALL **MADRID** RECEIVED WAS A BLANK PIECE OF PAPER! FORTUNATELY, THE MISTAKE WAS RECTIFIED AND THE TRANSFER COUP WAS COMPLETED.

FROM WHICH CLUBS DID **CITY** SIGN THE FOLLOWING BRAZILIANS?

**1**   **ELANO**, 2007

**2**   **MAICON**, 2012

**3**   **JÔ**, 2008

**4**   **FERNANDO**, 2014

**5**   **DOUGLAS LUIZ**, 2017

**6**   **GABRIEL JESUS**, 2016

**7**   **DANILO**, 2017

**8**   **SYLVINHO**, 2009

**9**   **EDERSON**, 2017

**10**   **GLÁUBER**, 2008

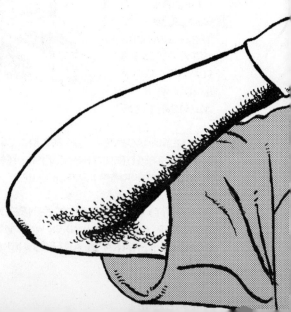

# THE CENTURIONS

AFTER IMPRESSING AS A U.S. COLLEGE STAR, *CLAUDIO REYNA* SPENT THE MAJORITY OF HIS CAREER IN EUROPE. HE JOINED *BAYER 04 LEVERKUSEN* AFTER THE 1994 WORLD CUP, MOVING ON TO *VFL WOLFSBURG*, WHERE HE BECAME THE FIRST AMERICAN TO CAPTAIN A EUROPEAN CLUB. A LEAGUE AND CUP DOUBLE WITH *RANGERS* WAS FOLLOWED BY A MOVE TO *SUNDERLAND*, BUT A KNEE INJURY RULED HIM OUT OF ACTION FOR MOST OF HIS SECOND SEASON WITH THE CLUB. INJURIES CONTINUED TO DOG HIM THROUGHOUT HIS TIME WITH *CITY*, AND HE RETURNED TO THE STATES IN 2007 TO JOIN *NEW YORK RED BULLS*.

NICKNAMED *"CAPTAIN AMERICA"* BY BRITISH FANS, *REYNA* PLAYED 112 TIMES FOR THE *UNITED STATES*. NAME THESE OTHER *CITY* CENTURIONS:

**1**   134 APPEARANCES FOR *REPUBLIC OF IRELAND*

**2**   112 APPEARANCES FOR *PARAGUAY*

**3**   100 APPEARANCES FOR *BRAZIL*

**4**   129 APPEARANCES FOR *DENMARK*

**5**   103 APPEARANCES FOR *CROATIA*

**6**   106 APPEARANCES FOR *ENGLAND*

**7**   129 APPEARANCES FOR *CHILE*

**8**   120 APPEARANCES FOR *IVORY COAST*

**9**   101 APPEARANCES FOR *IVORY COAST*

**10**   125 APPEARANCES FOR *SPAIN*

# TEN TYKES

THE £6,000 PAID TO **BARNSLEY** IN 1928 TO SIGN **ERIC BROOK** AND **FREDDIE TILSON** WAS ONE OF THE MOST ASTUTE BITS OF BUSINESS THAT **CITY** HAVE EVER DONE.

BETWEEN THEM, THE PAIR NETTED 310 GOALS IN A COMBINED APPEARANCE TOTAL OF 726 GAMES. HAD THE SECOND WORLD WAR NOT INTERVENED, **ENGLAND** WINGER **BROOK** MAY WELL HAVE ADDED TO HIS TOTAL OF 177 GOALS FOR **CITY**, A RECORD THAT STOOD FOR 78 YEARS UNTIL IT WAS BETTERED BY **SERGIO AGÜERO**. **BROOK'S** CAREER WAS ENDED BY THE FRACTURED SKULL HE RECEIVED IN A WARTIME CAR CRASH WHICH LEFT HIM UNABLE TO HEAD A BALL AGAIN.

IDENTIFY THESE **CITY** PLAYERS WHO ALSO PLAYED FOR **BARNSLEY**:

**1** LOANED OUT TO *BARNSLEY*, HE HAS GONE ON TO PLAY FOR *BURNLEY*, *SPURS*, *ATLÉTICO MADRID* AND *ENGLAND*.

**2** *NORTHERN IRELAND* DEFENDER, HE WAS A FAN FAVOURITE AT *BARNSLEY*, YO-YOED IN AND OUT OF THE PREMIER LEAGUE WITH *BOLTON WANDERERS*, WON A LEAGUE CUP AND PROMOTION WITH *LEICESTER CITY*, AND SPENT TIME WITH *STOKE CITY*.

**3** SON OF *NEWCASTLE UNITED*, *MANCHESTER UNITED*, *CITY* AND *ENGLAND* STRIKER *ANDY*, HE HAS PLAYED FOR CLUBS IN ENGLAND AND SCOTLAND AND RETURNED TO *BARNSLEY* IN 2021.

**4** *ENGLAND* DEFENDER WHO MADE HIS NAME AT *BARNSLEY* AND *EVERTON* BEFORE SIGNING FOR *CITY* IN 2016.

**5** PLAYED IN THE 1955 AND 1956 FA CUP FINALS, SCORING THE OPENING GOAL IN THE LATTER, AND WHEN HE LEFT *CITY* FOR *BARNSLEY* AFTER 12 YEARS, HIS 152 GOALS PLACED HIM THIRD ON *CITY'S* ALL-TIME GOALSCORING LIST AT THAT TIME.

**6** A MEMBER OF THE *CITY* TEAM THAT WON THAT 1999 DIVISION 2 PLAY OFF FINAL AT WEMBLEY STADIUM AGAINST *GILLINGHAM*, HE MOVED ON TO *BARNSLEY* AND PLAYED FOR A NUMBER OF CLUBS, BEFORE ENLISTING AS A GUNNER IN THE RAF REGIMENT!

**7** UNDERSTUDY TO *KEN MULHEARN* AND *HARRY DOWD* AT *CITY*, HE KEPT GOAL FOR *STOCKPORT COUNTY* FOR EIGHT YEARS.

**8** LEFT CITY IN 1986 FOR *BARNSLEY*, AN ATTACKING FULL BACK WHO WAS A REGULAR AT *PORTSMOUTH* AND THEN EXCELLED IN *KEVIN KEEGAN'S* PROMOTION-WINNING *NEWCASTLE UNITED* TEAM.

**9** HIS GOALSCORING EXPLOITS FOR *PRESTON NORTH END* EARNED A 2002 TRANSFER TO *CITY* BUT AFTER INJURY SETBACKS, HE WENT ON TO PLAY FOR A SUCCESSION OF CLUBS.

**10** MADE HIS REPUTATION AT *BARNSLEY*, GAINED PROMOTION TO THE TOP FLIGHT WITH *CITY*, WON A LEAGUE AND CUP DOUBLE WITH *CELTIC*, BEFORE A MANAGEMENT CAREER THAT SAW HIM TAKE THE *REPUBLIC OF IRELAND* TO THE 2002 WORLD CUP.

# "MAVERICK" MARSH

THE FLAMBOYANT *RODNEY MARSH* WON HONOURS WITH *QUEENS PARK RANGERS* AND *CITY* BEFORE EMBRACING FOOTBALL STATESIDE. BESIDES HIS PUNDITRY CREDITS, HE HAS RACKED UP APPEARANCES ON A NUMBER OF TV SHOWS, INCLUDING *"CELEBRITY COACH TRIP"*, *"CELEBRITY COME DINE WITH ME"*, *CASH IN THE ATTIC"* AND *"I'M A CELEBRITY...GET ME OUT OF HERE!"*

**1** WITH WHICH CLUB DID *RODNEY MARSH* MAKE HIS PROFESSIONAL DEBUT IN 1963?

**2** *MARSH* SIGNED FOR *QUEENS PARK RANGERS* IN 1966, WHERE HE WON TWO PROMOTIONS AND A LEAGUE CUP. WHO DID *QPR* BEAT 3-2 TO WIN THE 1967 LEAGUE CUP FINAL?

**3** HE JOINED *MANCHESTER CITY* IN 1972 FOR A THEN-CLUB RECORD FEE OF £200,000. NAME THE TEAM MANAGER WHO SIGNED HIM.

**4** *MARSH* WAS ON THE LOSING SIDE IN THE 1974 LEAGUE CUP FINAL WHEN *MANCHESTER CITY* WERE DEFEATED 2-1 BY WHICH TEAM?

**5** NAME THE THREE OTHER MANAGERS HE PLAYED UNDER BEFORE LEAVING *MANCHESTER CITY* IN EARLY 1976.

**6** HE MOVED TO THE U.S. IN 1976 TO PLAY FOR WHICH NASL TEAM?

**7** THE WINTER OF 1976 SAW *MARSH* PLAY ON LOAN BACK IN BRITAIN WITH *FULHAM*, ALONGSIDE WHICH SUPERSTAR NASL TEAMMATE?

**8** HIS 1976 SOJOURN WITH *FULHAM* SAW HIM REUNITED WITH -- AND PLAYING ONCE MORE FOR -- WHICH FORMER *QPR* MANAGER?

**9** NAME ONE OF THE THREE U.S. TEAMS *MARSH* COACHED.

**10** WHILE WORKING AS A *SKY SPORTS* PUNDIT, HE HONOURED HIS PLEDGE TO PUBLICLY SHAVE HIS HEAD IF WHICH CLUB MANAGED TO AVOID RELEGATION FROM THE PREMIER LEAGUE?

# CITY POTY

*JOE CORRIGAN* ROSE THROUGH THE RANKS AT *CITY* TO BECOME ONE OF THE CLUB'S GREATEST SERVANTS. HE PLAYED 16 SEASONS WITH THE SENIOR TEAM, DURING WHICH TIME HE EARNED NINE *ENGLAND* CAPS, BEFORE HEADING STATESIDE FOR A SPELL IN THE NASL. *JOE* RETURNED TO ENGLAND TO SIGN FOR *BRIGHTON & HOVE ALBION*, AND HAD LOAN SPELLS WITH *NORWICH CITY* AND *STOKE CITY*, BEFORE NECK PROBLEMS FORCED HIS RETIREMENT IN 1985.

*JOE* WAS VOTED *CITY PLAYER OF THE YEAR* THREE TIMES. IDENTIFY THESE OTHER WINNERS OF THE AWARD:

**1** NAME THE THREE SCOTTISH PLAYERS WHO HAVE WON THE AWARD SINCE IT WAS FIRST INTRODUCED IN 1967.

**2** NAME THE FOUR *REPUBLIC OF IRELAND* INTERNATIONALS WHO HAVE WON THE PLAYER OF THE YEAR AWARD.

**3** WHO IS THE ONLY ALGERIAN TO WIN THE AWARD?

**4** WHO IS THE ONLY OTHER GOALKEEPER VOTED POTY?

**5** WHICH DUTCH PLAYER, WHO IN EACH OF HIS FIVE SEASONS WITH THE BLUES WAS EITHER PROMOTED OR RELEGATED, WON IN 1999?

**6** THREE *ARGENTINA* INTERNATIONALS WON THE AWARD -- *PABLO ZABALETA, SERGIO AGÜERO* AND *CARLOS TEVEZ* -- BUT WHO WAS THE ONLY ONE OF THEM TO WIN TWICE?

**7** WHO IS THE ONLY GERMAN TO WIN THE AWARD?

**8** WHICH *BELGIAN* INTERNATIONAL WON MORE AWARDS -- *VINCENT KOMPANY* OR *KEVIN DE BRUYNE?*

**9** WHICH FRENCH PLAYER WON IN 2003?

**10** WHICH WINNER OF THE 1973 FA CUP WITH SUNDERLAND WON THE AWARD IN 1977 -- *DENNIS TUEART* OR *DAVE WATSON?*

# "IT'S HAMMER TIME!"

**PABLO ZABALETA** REJECTED AN OFFER FROM **JUVENTUS** BECAUSE HE HAD LONG DREAMED OF PLAYING IN THE PREMIER LEAGUE. THE ARGENTINIAN FULL-BACK MADE HIS **CITY** DEBUT ON THE SAME DAY AS **ROBINHO**, AND WHILE THE SEEMINGLY DISINTERESTED BRAZILIAN DISAPPOINTED AND WAS SOON GONE, **ZABALETA'S** BRAVERY AND UNCOMPROMISING COMMITMENT, TEMPERED WITH HIS OBVIOUS PASSION FOR THE CLUB, MADE HIM BELOVED BY THE **CITY** FAITHFUL. AFTER NINE SEASONS AND 333 GAMES, HE JOINED **WEST HAM UNITED** IN 2017:

THE FOLLOWING ALSO PLAYED FOR BOTH **CITY** AND **WEST HAM:**

**1** **ENGLAND** GOALKEEPER WHO BEGAN HIS CAREER WITH **SHREWSBURY TOWN** AND WON FOUR GOLDEN GLOVES WITH **CITY**.

**2** THE FIRST BLACK PLAYER TO COMMAND A £1 MILLION FEE WITH HIS TRANSFER FROM **NORWICH CITY** TO **NOTTINGHAM FOREST**, AND THE FIRST TOP FLIGHT PLAYER TO BE OPENLY GAY.

**3** HE MADE HIS NAME WITH **NORTHAMPTON TOWN** AND ONCE MISSED EIGHT GAMES FOR **WEST HAM** WHEN HE WAS STABBED BY HIS WIFE!

**4** FORMER **SOUTHAMPTON** AND **CHELSEA** FULL BACK, AN **ENGLAND** INTERNATIONAL WHO MARRIED POP STAR **FRANKIE SANDFORD** OF **THE SATURDAYS** IN 2014.

**5** **NORTHERN IRELAND** INTERNATIONAL WHO PLAYED IN THREE DIVISIONS FOR **CITY** AND SCORED THE FIRST GOAL OF THE FABLED PLAY-OFF FINAL COMEBACK AGAINST **GILLINGHAM** IN 1999.

**6** SCOUSER WHO BECAME A **WEST HAM** CULT HERO IN BETWEEN TWO SPELLS WITH **CITY**, THE SECOND OF WHICH SAW HIM LEAVE FOR **MIAMI FUSION** IN 2001 AFTER BACK-TO-BACK PROMOTIONS.

**7** **NORTHERN IRELAND** INTERNATIONAL, SCORED AN OWN GOAL IN THE INFAMOUS 2-2 DRAW AGAINST **LIVERPOOL** THAT SAW **CITY** RELEGATED IN 1996, HE BECAME CLUB CAPTAIN AT **WEST HAM**.

**8** FIERY WELSH INTERNATIONAL WHO WON HONOURS WITH *CELTIC, LIVERPOOL* AND *CARDIFF CITY.*

**9** *ENGLAND* WINGER, HE WAS *BLACKPOOL'S* YOUNGEST DEBUTANT TO THAT POINT, A CROWD FAVOURITE AT *QPR* AND *WEST HAM,* AND SCORER OF *CITY'S* FIRST COMPETITIVE GOAL AT *THE ETIHAD.*

**10** JOURNEYMAN STRIKER WHO WAS *WEST HAM'S* RECORD SIGNING IN 1977, HE WON THE FA CUP WITH *"THE HAMMERS"* BEFORE JOINING *CITY* IN 1982 AS THE REPLACEMENT FOR *TREVOR FRANCIS.*

# BIG MAL

**MIKE SUMMERBEE** DESCRIBED **MALCOLM ALLISON** AS *"THE GREATEST COACH THIS COUNTRY EVER HAD"*. **DON REVIE** SAID HE WAS AN *"EMBARRASSMENT TO THE GAME"* AND **BRIAN CLOUGH** DUBBED HIM THE *"ERROL FLYNN OF FOOTBALL"*. AS ASSISTANT TO **JOE MERCER**, HE WAS THE TACTICAL VISIONARY WHO MASTERMINDED **CITY'S** SUCCESS IN THE LATE 1960S. BUT WHEN A BOARDROOM COUP SAW **MERCER** BOOTED UPSTAIRS AND **ALLISON** INSTALLED AT THE HELM, **"BIG MAL"** WAS FOUND WANTING. SUBSEQUENTLY, THE FEDORA-SPORTING FLAMBOYANCE, THEATRICS AND PURSUIT OF THE HIGH LIFE OVERSHADOWED ANY FOOTBALLING ACHIEVEMENTS.

**1** HAVING LAUNCHED HIS CAREER AT **CHARLTON ATHLETIC**, **ALLISON** WON PROMOTION WITH WHICH LONDON CLUB?

**2** WHAT WAS THE DISEASE THAT CURTAILED HIS PLAYING CAREER?

**3** NAME ONE OF THE CLUBS HE MANAGED BEFORE BECOMING ASSISTANT MANAGER OF **MANCHESTER CITY** IN 1965.

**4** HE BECAME MANAGER OF WHICH LONDON CLUB IN 1973?

**5** **ALLISON** MANAGED WHICH TURKISH CLUB IN THE MID-1970S?

**6** HE RETURNED TO MANAGE **CITY** AGAIN IN 1979 WHEN APPOINTED BY WHICH CLUB CHAIRMAN?

**7** DURING THAT SECOND SPELL IN CHARGE, HE BROKE THE BRITISH TRANSFER RECORD TO SIGN WHICH **WOLVERHAMPTON WANDERERS** MIDFIELDER FOR £1,437,500?

**8** **MALCOLM'S** SUCCESSOR AT **CITY** IN 1980 WAS WHICH MANAGER HE HAD MENTORED DURING THEIR PLAYING DAYS TOGETHER?

**9** **ALLISON** WON LEAGUE AND CUP HONOURS WITH WHICH PORTUGUESE CLUB IN THE EARLY 1980S?

**10** HE MANAGED THE NATIONAL TEAM OF WHICH COUNTRY?

# ROQUE OF THE ROVERS

*ROQUE SANTA CRUZ* WAS BORN IN ASUNCIÓN, PARAGUAY, ON AUGUST 16, 1981. HE MADE HIS SENIOR DEBUT FOR *CLUB OLIMPIA* AT THE AGE OF 15 AND WON THREE CONSECUTIVE LEAGUE TITLES. FOLLOWING OUTSTANDING PERFORMANCES FOR *PARAGUAY* AT THE UNDER-20 WORLD CUP AND IN THE COPA AMERICA, 17-YEAR-OLD *"BABY GOAL"* JOINED *BAYERN MUNICH* IN 1999, GOING ON TO WIN FIVE LEAGUE TITLES AND THE UEFA CHAMPIONS LEAGUE. HE RETURNED TO *CLUB OLIMPIA* IN 2016, WHERE HE HAS ADDED NUMEROUS HONOURS TO HIS INITIAL TALLY.

*SANTA CRUZ* WAS MANAGED BY *MARK HUGHES* AT *BLACKBURN ROVERS* AND THEY WERE REUNITED AT *CITY*. IDENTIFY THESE OTHERS WHO HAVE PLAYED FOR BOTH *BLACKBURN ROVERS* AND *CITY*:

**1** CITY'S PLAYER OF THE YEAR IN 1993, HE SPENT TEN YEARS AT *BLACKBURN*, MANY AS CAPTAIN, WHERE HE EXPERIENCED PROMOTION AND RELEGATIONS AND WON THE 2002 LEAGUE CUP.

**2** AFTER WINNING PROMOTION AND REACHING AN FA CUP FINAL WITH *ROVERS*, HE WAS SIGNED AS *DENIS LAW'S* REPLACEMENT IN 1961 AND FINISHED THE SEASON AS *CITY'S* TOP SCORER. FOLLOWING RELEGATION THE NEXT SEASON, HE WAS SOLD TO NEWLY PROMOTED *STOKE CITY*, WITH WHOM HE WON THE 1972 LEAGUE CUP.

**3** 6' 5" CENTRE-BACK, LOANED OUT TO *BLACKBURN* AND *WEST BROMWICH ALBION*, BEFORE SIGNING FOR *FULHAM* IN 2020.

**4** CAPTAINED *SCOTLAND* AT THE 1998 WORLD CUP AND WON LEAGUE TITLES WITH *BLACKBURN* AND *RANGERS*.

**5** PLAYED IN THE 1981 CUP FINAL FOR *CITY*, WON PROMOTION WITH *BLACKBURN* AND A LEAGUE CUP WITH *SLIGO*, BEFORE BECOMING A PHYSIOTHERAPIST WITH *CITY* AND *BURY* AMONG OTHERS.

**6** *FAROE ISLANDS* GOALKEEPER.

**7** *ZIMBABWE* INTERNATIONAL STRIKER.

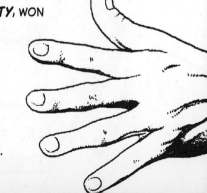

**8** PLAYED UNDER *HUGHES* AT *BLACKBURN* AND *CITY*, WON HONOURS AT NUMEROUS CLUBS, INCLUDING WINNING THE 2013 CHAMPIONSHIP WITH HIS FINAL CLUB, *CARDIFF CITY*.

**9** 1993 PREMIER LEAGUE GOLDEN BOOT WINNER, EARNED HONOURS WITH *ARSENAL*, *NEWCASTLE UNITED*, *MANCHESTER UNITED* AND *BLACKBURN* AND WAS CAPPED 15 TIMES BY *ENGLAND*.

**10** SCORED THE 1999 INJURY TIME EQUALISER AGAINST *GILLINGHAM* THAT WAS VOTED *CITY'S* GREATEST-EVER GOAL IN A 2005 POLL.

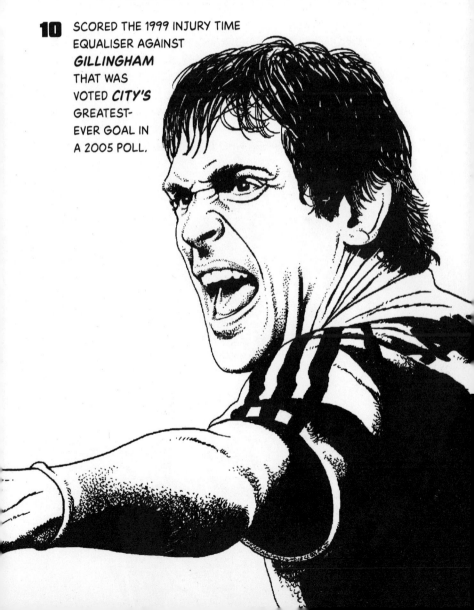

# "NIALL QUINN'S DISCO PANTS ARE THE BEST"

ON A PRE-SEASON TOUR OF ITALY, THE TEAM'S SANCTIONED NIGHT OUT ON THE TOWN CULMINATED IN A SHIRTLESS *NIALL QUINN* DOING SOME FRENETIC DANCING IN A DISCO BAR. HE WAS SPOTTED BY A GROUP OF *CITY* FANS AND A LEGENDARY TERRACE CHANT WAS BORN. THE PAEAN TO THE IRISH STRIKER AND HIS CUT-OFF JEANS WAS SO POPULAR THAT IT FOLLOWED HIM THROUGHOUT HIS CAREER AND WAS EVEN RELEASED AS A SINGLE -- *"NIALL QUINN'S DISCO PANTS"* BY *SUNDERLAND* FANS *A LOVE SUPREME* -- THAT REACHED NO. 56 IN THE CHARTS IN 1999.

**1**   *QUINN* BEGAN HIS TOP-FLIGHT CAREER WITH WHICH LONDON CLUB?

**2**   WHO WAS THE *CITY* MANAGER WHO SIGNED *QUINN* IN 1990?

**3**  NAME TWO OF THE FOUR OTHER MANAGERS UNDER WHOM *QUINN* PLAYED DURING HIS SIX YEARS WITH *CITY*.

**4**  *NIALL QUINN* ONCE WENT IN GOAL AND SAVED A PENALTY, IN A 2-1 WIN OVER *DERBY COUNTY*, FOLLOWING THE DISMISSAL OF WHICH *CITY* GOALKEEPER?

**5**  AT *SUNDERLAND*, HE STRUCK UP A PROLIFIC PARTNERSHIP WITH WHICH PLAYER THAT EARNED HIS TEAMMATE THE GOLDEN BOOT?

**6**  *NIALL'S* GOAL AGAINST *CYPRUS* ON HIS 35TH BIRTHDAY MADE HIM THE *REPUBLIC OF IRELAND'S* ALL-TIME TOP GOALSCORER TO THAT POINT, BREAKING THE RECORD SET BY WHICH *ARSENAL* AND *MANCHESTER UNITED* STRIKER?

**7**  HE REMAINED THE *REPUBLIC OF IRELAND'S* ALL-TIME TOP GOALSCORER UNTIL THAT RECORD WAS BROKEN BY WHICH STRIKER?

**8**  IN WHICH TWO WORLD CUP TOURNAMENTS DID *NIALL QUINN* REPRESENT HIS COUNTRY?

**9**  UNDER WHICH FORMER *MANCHESTER CITY* MANAGER DID *NIALL QUINN* PLAY AT *SUNDERLAND?*

**10**  *QUINN* HEADED UP THE *DRUMAVILLE CONSORTIUM* THAT BOUGHT THE CONTROLLING INTEREST IN *SUNDERLAND* IN 2006 -- WHO WAS THE AMERICAN BUSINESSMAN WHO REPLACED HIM AS CHAIRMAN OF THE CLUB IN 2011?

# TOGO'S GO-TO GUY

THE ALL-TIME TOP GOALSCORER FOR THE *TOGO* NATIONAL TEAM AND HOLDER OF THE APPEARANCES RECORD FOR HIS COUNTRY, *EMMANUEL ADEBAYOR* WAS THE FIRST TOGOLESE PLAYER TO BE NAMED AFRICAN FOOTBALLER OF THE YEAR WHEN HE WON THE AWARD IN 2008. HE RETIRED FROM INTERNATIONAL FOOTBALL FOLLOWING A DEADLY TERRORIST ATTACK ON THE *TOGO* TEAM BUS AT THE 2010 AFRICAN CUP OF NATIONS, BUT LATER RELENTED AND CONTINUED TO PLAY FOR THE TEAM.

**1** HAVING MADE HIS NAME IN FRANCE WITH *METZ*, HE REACHED THE FINAL OF THE UEFA CHAMPIONS LEAGUE WITH WHICH FRENCH CLUB?

**2** HE JOINED *CITY* FROM *ARSENAL* IN 2009. WHAT NUMBER SHIRT DID HE WEAR WITH *"THE GUNNERS"* AND INITIALLY AT *CITY?*

**3** WHO WAS THE MANAGER WHO SIGNED *ADEBAYOR* TO *CITY?*

**4** HE SCORED IN EACH OF HIS FIRST FOUR GAMES FOR *CITY*, INCLUDING THE VICTORY OVER *ARSENAL* THAT SAW HIM RUN THE LENGTH OF THE PITCH TO CELEBRATE IN FRONT OF INCENSED *ARSENAL* FANS. WHAT WAS THE SCORE IN THAT GAME?

**5** THAT SAME GAME FEATURED AN INCIDENT THAT RESULTED IN A THREE-GAME BAN FOR *ADEBAYOR* AFTER HE WAS RETROACTIVELY FOUND GUILTY OF VIOLENT CONDUCT AGAINST WHICH FORMER *ARSENAL* TEAMMATE?

**6** HE SCORED HIS FIRST HAT-TRICK FOR *CITY* IN A UEFA EUROPA LEAGUE GROUP STAGE MATCH AGAINST WHICH POLISH TEAM?

**7** SENT OUT ON LOAN IN EARLY 2011, HE WON A COPA DEL REY WITH **REAL MADRID**, WHO WERE THEN MANAGED BY WHICH COACH?

**8** HE WENT ON TO PLAY FOR WHICH TWO LONDON CLUBS?

**9** NAME ONE OF THE TWO COUNTRIES IN WHICH **ADEBAYOR** SUBSEQUENTLY PLAYED BETWEEN 2017 AND 2020.

**10** **ADEBAYOR** PLAYED FOR **TOGO** IN THE COUNTRY'S FIRST-EVER APPEARANCE AT THE WORLD CUP -- IN WHICH YEAR?

# THE BHOYS ARE BACK IN TOWN

CAPPED 81 TIMES BY *GREECE, GEORGIOS SAMARAS* WAS BORN IN HERAKLION, THE CAPITAL OF THE ISLAND OF CRETE. HE BEGAN HIS CAREER AT LOCAL CLUB *OFI CRETE*, AND AFTER PLAYING FOR CLUBS IN THE NETHERLANDS, ENGLAND, SCOTLAND, SAUDI ARABIA, THE USA, SPAIN AND TURKEY, RETURNED HOME TO BECOME *OFI CRETE* VICE-PRESIDENT.

AFTER LEAVING *CITY*, HE FOUND HIS GREATEST SUCCESS WITH *CELTIC*, WITH WHOM HE WON FOUR LEAGUE TITLES AND THREE CUPS. IDENTIFY THESE OTHER INTERNATIONALS WHO PLAYED FOR *CITY* AND *CELTIC*.

**1** *IVORY COAST* DEFENDER WHO WON LEAGUE TITLES WITH *ARSENAL, CITY* AND *CELTIC* AND REACHED THE 2016 EUROPA LEAGUE FINAL WITH *LIVERPOOL*.

**2** *BELGIUM* DEFENDER, *CITY'S* YOUNG PLAYER OF THE YEAR IN 2009-10, SPENT TIME ON LOAN AT *BOLTON* AND *FC TWENTE* BEFORE JOINING *CELTIC* IN 2015. HE SIGNED FOR *HERTHA BSC* IN 2019.

**3** CAPPED 78 TIMES BY *ISRAEL*, HIS TRAVELS TOOK HIM TO *SOUTHAMPTON, WEST HAM, CELTIC, BLACKBURN, CITY, PORTSMOUTH* AND BACK TO HIS FIRST CLUB, *MACCABI HAIFA*.

**4** *NORTHERN IRELAND* INTERNATIONAL WHO MADE JUST ONE APPEARANCE FOR *CITY* BEFORE PLAYING FOR *CREWE ALEXANDRA, LEICESTER CITY, CELTIC, NOTTINGHAM FOREST* AND *WYCOMBE WANDERERS*, WINNING MULTIPLE HONOURS IN TWO SPELLS AS *CELTIC* BOSS, MANAGING *BOLTON WANDERERS* AND WINNING THE CHAMPIONSHIP WITH *HIBERNIAN*.

**5** GOALKEEPER CAPPED 134 TIMES BY *REPUBLIC OF IRELAND*.

**6** *SWEDEN* STRIKER WHO SCORED 20 GOALS IN 23 GAMES ON LOAN FROM *CITY* AT *FEYENOORD*, BEFORE WINNING A LEAGUE AND CUP DOUBLE WHILE ON LOAN AT *CELTIC*.

**7** CAPPED 78 TIMES BY *WALES* BETWEEN 1998 AND 2013.

**8** **BELGIUM** DEFENDER WHO, WHILE ON LOAN FROM **CITY**, WON A LEAGUE AND CUP DOUBLE WITH **CELTIC** IN 2015, LEAGUE AND CUP HONOURS IN TWO SPELLS WITH **GALATASARAY**, AND WAS RELEGATED WITH **SUNDERLAND** -- BEFORE JOINING **OLYMPIQUE LYONNAIS** AND KNOCKING **CITY** OUT OF EUROPE IN 2020.

**9** **SWANSEA CITY** STAR WINGER WHO STRUGGLED TO MAKE A BREAKTHROUGH AT **CITY** BEFORE MOVING ON TO ASTON VILLA. HE WON NUMEROUS HONOURS WITH **CELTIC**, INCLUDING TWO TREBLES AND BOTH THE PFA SCOTLAND PLAYERS' PLAYER OF THE YEAR AND SFWA FOOTBALLER OF THE YEAR AWARDS. CAPPED AT EVERY LEVEL EXCEPT SENIOR BY **ENGLAND**, HE PLAYED IN THE 2012 **GREAT BRITAIN** OLYMPIC TEAM.

**10** WON HONOURS WITH **BARNSLEY**, **CITY** AND **CELTIC**, HE WAS CAPPED 57 TIMES BY THE **REPUBLIC OF IRELAND**, WHOM HE LATER MANAGED IN TWO SEPARATE SPELLS.

# THE HAPPY WANDERERS

CAPPED 59 TIMES BY *GERMANY*, *DIETMAR HAMANN* SPENT THE MAJORITY OF HIS CAREER IN ENGLISH FOOTBALL AFTER LEAVING *BAYERN MUNICH* FOR *NEWCASTLE UNITED* IN 1998. HE EARNED MULTIPLE HONOURS WITH *LIVERPOOL*, INCLUDING THE UEFA CHAMPIONS LEAGUE AND UEFA CUP, THEN JOINED *BOLTON WANDERERS* -- BUT CHANGED HIS MIND ONE DAY LATER AND SIGNED FOR *CITY!* FOLLOWING A SPELL WITH *MK DONS* AS A PLAYER/COACH, HE COACHED AT *LEICESTER CITY* BEFORE ENTERING MANAGEMENT WITH *STOCKPORT COUNTY*.

IDENTIFY THESE *CITY* PLAYERS WHO DIDN'T CHANGE THEIR MINDS ABOUT JOINING *BOLTON WANDERERS*:

**1** BULGARIAN FOOTBALLER OF THE YEAR, A WINGER WHO SPENT THREE SEASONS WITH *CITY* BEFORE JOINING *BOLTON* IN 2010.

**2** *SLOVAKIA* INTERNATIONAL WHO, DURING HIS THREE SEASONS WITH *CITY*, WAS LOANED OUT TO *BOLTON* AND *ESPANYOL* AND WON THE 2010 LEAGUE AND CUP DOUBLE WITH *RANGERS*.

**3** STRIKER WHOSE CLUBS INCLUDED *BOLTON*, *NEWCASTLE UNITED*, *CITY*, *MANCHESTER UNITED* AND *STOCKPORT COUNTY*, HE EARNED *WALES* CAPS BETWEEN 1963 AND 1973.

**4** *ENGLAND* STAR OF THE 1980S AND '90S, HE HAD TWO SPELLS WITH HIS BELOVED *NEWCASTLE UNITED* -- WHERE HE WOULD LATER COACH AND BE ASSISTANT MANAGER -- AND PLAYED FOR BOTH LIVERPOOL CLUBS, BOTH MANCHESTER CLUBS, *BOLTON* AND MORE.

**5** SIGNED TO *CITY* FROM *BOLTON* IN 1967 FOR A RECORD £60,000.

**6** *BELGIUM* INTERNATIONAL DEFENDER WHO SPENT THE 2011-12 SEASON ON LOAN WITH *BOLTON* BEFORE WINNING MULTIPLE HONOURS WITH *CELTIC* AND THEN JOINED *HERTHA BSC*.

**7** SON OF A *CITY* LEGEND, HE HAD TWO SPELLS AT *CITY*, TWO SPELLS AT *SWINDON TOWN*, PLAYED FOR *BOLTON*, *LEICESTER CITY* AND *BRADFORD CITY* AND WON PROMOTION WITH *SUNDERLAND*.

**8** DEFENSIVE MIDFIELDER WHO WON PROMOTIONS WITH *MIDDLESBROUGH* AND BOLTON BEFORE JOINING *CITY* IN 1998, WHERE HIS OWN GOAL CONDEMNED *CITY* TO RELEGATION TO THE THIRD TIER FOR THE FIRST TIME IN THE CLUB'S HISTORY.

**9** SCOTTISH MIDFIELDER WITH *TOTTENHAM HOTSPUR, BOLTON* AND *BRIGHTON & HOVE ALBION,* HE WAS TWICE NAMED *CITY* PLAYER OF THE YEAR AND INSPIRED THE TEAM'S 1989 PROMOTION.

**10** PLAYED FOR AND LATER COACHED BOTH MANCHESTER CLUBS, PLAYED FOR *ARSENAL, EVERTON, BOLTON* AND *FORT LAUDERDALE STRIKERS* AND MANAGED *BLACKBURN ROVERS.*

# CAPTAIN KID

CAPTAIN OF THE TEAM THAT WON THE 1986 FA YOUTH CUP, *STEVE REDMOND* WAS A FIRST TEAM REGULAR AT 18, AND WAS NAMED CLUB PLAYER OF THE YEAR IN 1988, THE SAME YEAR HE BECAME *CITY'S* YOUNGEST-EVER CAPTAIN AND MADE HIS *ENGLAND U-21* DEBUT. HE PLAYED EVERY SINGLE GAME IN THREE CONSECUTIVE SEASONS FOR CITY.

**1** ALONGSIDE *PAUL LAKE, ANDY HINCHCLIFFE* AND *IAN BRIGHTWELL, REDMOND* PLAYED FOR WHICH *CITY* FEEDER TEAM BASED IN CHEADLE?

**2** HE CAPTAINED THE 1986 SIDE THAT WON THE FA YOUTH CUP FOR THE FIRST TIME IN *CITY'S* HISTORY. WHO MANAGED THAT TEAM?

**3** *REDMOND* PLAYED IN CITY'S BIGGEST WIN OF THE 20TH CENTURY, A 10-1 THRASHING OF WHICH OPPONENTS IN NOVEMBER, 1987?

**4** NAME THE THREE PLAYERS WHO SCORED HAT-TRICKS FOR *CITY* IN THAT 10-1 VICTORY.

**5** *REDMOND* TOOK OVER IN GOAL AGAINST *CRYSTAL PALACE* THAT SEASON FOLLOWING THE DISMISSAL OF WHICH GOALKEEPER, A MUCH-TRAVELLED PLAYER WHO HAD 13 CLUBS *(INCLUDING 13 YEARS WITH TRANMERE ROVERS)* IN HIS 22-YEAR CAREER?

**6** HE PLAYED IN THE FAMOUS 5-1 THRASHING OF *MANCHESTER UNITED* IN SEPTEMBER 1989 -- WHO GOT *CITY'S* GOALS THAT DAY?

**7** *STEVE* REPLACED WHICH DEFENDER -- WHO LEFT HIS SECOND SPELL AT *CITY* TO JOIN *BURY* -- AS CLUB CAPTAIN?

**8** *REDMOND* LEFT *CITY* IN 1992 TO JOIN WHICH NORTH-WEST CLUB?

**9** NAME THE SIX MANAGERS HE PLAYED FOR AT *CITY* BETWEEN HIS 1986 DEBUT AND HIS DEPARTURE IN THE SUMMER OF 1992.

**10** HE WAS JOINT CARETAKER-MANAGER, AND SUBSEQUENTLY PLAYER/ ASSISTANT MANAGER, WITH *ANDY PREECE* AT WHICH CLUB?

# BIG MEEKS

WHEN HE MADE HIS FULL INTERNATIONAL DEBUT IN 2006, *MICAH RICHARDS* BECAME *ENGLAND'S* YOUNGEST-EVER DEFENDER. BORN IN BIRMINGHAM, RAISED IN LEEDS, HE PLAYED JUNIOR FOOTBALL WITH *LEEDS UNITED* AND *OLDHAM ATHLETIC,* BEFORE JOINING *CITY* AS A 14-YEAR-OLD. AFTER INITIALLY STRUGGLING TO GET A YTS CONTRACT, HE MADE HIS LEAGUE DEBUT FOR *CITY* AT THE AGE OF 17.

**1** AN EXHILARATED *MICAH* FAMOUSLY SWORE IN A POST-GAME INTERVIEW ON LIVE TV AFTER SCORING HIS FIRST GOAL FOR *CITY* IN A 2006 FA CUP TIE AGAINST WHICH OPPONENTS?

**2** IN THE SUMMER OF 2009 HE WAS FORCED TO ISOLATE AFTER CATCHING WHICH DISEASE ON HOLIDAY IN AYIA NAPA, CYPRUS?

**3** WHEN *MICAH* BECAME ENGLAND'S YOUNGEST-EVER DEFENDER, HE BROKE THE RECORD SET BY WHICH *WEST HAM UNITED, LEEDS UNITED* AND *MANCHESTER UNITED* STAR?

**4** *MICAH* MADE HIS FIRST 11 APPEARANCES FOR *ENGLAND* UNDER WHICH MANAGER?

**5** THE NEXT *ENGLAND* MANAGER, DURING HIS FOUR-YEAR TENURE, SNUBBED *RICHARDS*, RESTRICTING HIM TO JUST ONE APPEARANCE AS A SUBSTITUTE. WHO WAS THAT MANAGER?

**6** *RICHARDS* EARNED HIS 13TH AND FINAL *ENGLAND* CAP IN 2012, WHEN HE WAS SELECTED BY WHICH CARETAKER MANAGER?

**7** HE WAS SELECTED AS ONE OF THREE OVER-AGED PLAYERS TO REPRESENT *GREAT BRITAIN* AT THE 2012 OLYMPICS. WHO WERE THE OTHER TWO OVER-AGED PLAYERS -- ONE FROM *LIVERPOOL* AND THE OTHER FROM *MANCHESTER UNITED?*

**8** AFTER WINNING LEAGUE AND FA CUP HONOURS WITH *CITY*, HE FAILED TO MAKE ENOUGH APPEARANCES TO QUALIFY FOR A PREMIER LEAGUE WINNER'S MEDAL IN 2013-14 AND SUBSEQUENTLY JOINED WHICH ITALIAN CLUB ON A SEASON-LONG LOAN?

**9** HE ENDED HIS PLAYING CAREER WITH FOUR INJURY-PLAGUED SEASONS AT WHICH CLUB BEFORE RETIRING AT THE AGE OF 31?

**10** DURING THE 2020 EUROS, WHICH WERE DEFERRED TO 2021, *MICAH* WAS TEAMED WITH WHICH FORMER *MANCHESTER UNITED* STAR IN THE TV SERIES *"ROAD TO WEMBLEY"*?

# CITY'S CELEBS

ALL THREE MEMBERS OF CHART-TOPPERS *DOVES* -- *JIMI GOODWIN*, *JEZ WILLIAMS* AND *ANDY WILLIAMS*, AS WELL AS THE BAND'S MANAGER, *DAVE ROFE* -- ARE *CITY* FANS, AS ARE OTHER MUSICIANS, INCLUDING *NOEL* AND *LIAM GALLAGHER*, *BADLY DRAWN BOY*, *JOHNNY MARR* AND *MIKE PICKERING*.

IDENTIFY THE FOLLOWING CELEBRITY BLUES:

**1** REAL NAME *EDWARD MCGINNIS*, HE TEAMED UP WITH *CYRIL MEAD* TO CREATE A FAMOUS COMEDY DOUBLE ACT.

**2** ACCLAIMED ROCK PHOTOGRAPHER RENOWNED FOR HIS ICONIC IMAGES OF *JOY DIVISION*.

**3** *CURLY WATTS* IN *"CORONATION STREET"*.

**4** *BBC RADIO 6* DEEJAY, ONCE A MEMBER OF *THE FALL*, AND ONE HALF OF THE RADIO PAIRING *MARK AND LARD*.

**5** WORLD LIGHT-WELTERWEIGHT AND WELTERWEIGHT BOXING CHAMPION, NICKNAMED *"THE HITMAN"*.

**6** FOUNDER, COMPOSER AND KEYBOARDIST WITH THE DUO *SWING OUT SISTER*, FORMERLY OF *A CERTAIN RATIO*.

**7** AKA *JAMES BOND* AND *MR. PRICKLEPANTS*.

**8** LEAD GUITARIST WITH *THE CULT*.

**9** ALIAS *HANS GRUBER*, *THE SHERIFF OF NOTTINGHAM* AND *PROFESSOR SEVERUS SNAPE*.

**10** MANAGER OF *JOY DIVISION* AND *NEW ORDER*, CO-OWNER OF *FACTORY RECORDS* AND *THE HAÇIENDA*.

# THE STOCKPORT INIESTA

STOCKPORT-BORN **PHIL FODEN** JOINED **CITY** WHEN HE WAS FOUR YEARS OLD. TIPPED FOR STARDOM FROM AN EARLY AGE, UNDER THE GUIDANCE OF **PEP GUARDIOLA** HE HAS EMERGED AS ONE OF THE WORLD'S MOST COVETED YOUNG PLAYERS, A FULL **ENGLAND** INTERNATIONAL AND WINNER OF A PLETHORA OF HONOURS BEFORE HIS 21ST BIRTHDAY.

**1** HE SCORED TWICE IN THE FINAL OF THE 2017 FIFA U-17 WORLD CUP AS **ENGLAND** DEFEATED WHICH NATION TO BECOME CHAMPIONS?

**2** **FODEN** WON THE GOLDEN BALL AS MOST VALUABLE PLAYER AT THAT TOURNAMENT. WHO IS THE ONLY OTHER **CITY** PLAYER TO WIN THAT AWARD, PLAYING FOR CHAMPIONS **NIGERIA** IN 2013?

**3** HE MADE HIS FIRST TEAM DEBUT FOR **CITY**, COMING ON AS A SUBSTITUTE IN A UEFA CHAMPIONS LEAGUE GAME AGAINST **FEYENOORD** IN LATE 2017. TWO WEEKS LATER, AGAINST **SHAKHTAR DONETSK**, HE BECAME THE YOUNGEST PLAYER TO START A CHAMPIONS LEAGUE GAME, BREAKING THE RECORD SET BY **JOSH MCEACHRAN** WHILE PLAYING FOR WHICH TEAM?

**4** IN 2018, **FODEN** CAME ON AS SUBSTITUTE FOR **SERGIO AGÜERO** IN THE 3-0 EFL CUP FINAL VICTORY OVER WHICH OPPONENTS?

**5** LATER THAT YEAR, HE SCORED HIS FIRST SENIOR GOAL FOR **CITY** IN A 3RD ROUND EFL CUP WIN OVER WHICH CLUB?

**6** HE SCORED HIS FIRST PREMIER LEAGUE GOAL IN THE 1-0 WIN OVER **TOTTENHAM HOTSPUR** IN APRIL, 2019, BECOMING **CITY'S** THIRD-YOUNGEST PREMIER LEAGUE GOALSCORER BEHIND WHICH TWO FORMER **CITY** PLAYERS?

**7** WHAT WAS **PHIL FODEN'S** FIRST LOSS IN A FINAL DURING HIS SENIOR CAREER?

**8** **FODEN** WAS ONE OF TWO PLAYERS WITHDRAWN FROM THE **ENGLAND** SQUAD IN SEPTEMBER, 2020, FOR BREAKING COVID-19 ISOLATION PROTOCOLS -- WHO WAS THE OTHER PLAYER?

**9** HE SCORED HIS FIRST AND SECOND GOALS FOR *ENGLAND* IN A 4-0 WIN OVER WHICH COUNTRY AT WEMBLEY IN LATE 2020?

**10** HE WAS NAMED PFA YOUNG PLAYER OF THE YEAR IN 2021. NAME THREE OTHER *CITY* PLAYERS WHO HAVE WON THE AWARD DURING THEIR CAREERS.

# CATALAN CONNECTIONS

*CHILE'S* MOST-CAPPED GOALKEEPER, *CLAUDIO BRAVO* WAS BORN IN VILUCO ON APRIL 13, 1983. HE MADE HIS NAME AT *COLO-COLO*, WHERE HE WAS ORIGINALLY A STRIKER UNTIL HE PERSUADED HIS COACH TO LET HIM TRY OUT AS A GOALKEEPER. HE WAS GIVEN THE NICKNAME *"CÓNDOR CHICO"* -- WHICH MEANS *"LITTLE CONDOR"*. HE JOINED *CITY* FROM *BARCELONA* IN 2016.

IDENTIFY THESE *CITY* AND *BARCELONA* LINKS:

**1** HIS HONOURS INCLUDE THREE PREMIER LEAGUE TITLES WITH *CITY* AFTER SIGNING IN 2010 FROM *BARCELONA*, WITH WHOM HE WON TWO LA LIGA TITLES, THE UEFA CHAMPIONS LEAGUE AND MORE.

**2** JOINED *BARCELONA* ON A FREE TRANSFER AFTER WINNING FIVE PREMIER LEAGUE TITLES AND MORE WITH *CITY*.

**3** YOUNG SPANIARD SIGNED FOR £900,000 IN 2011 FROM *CELTA VIGO*, HE WAS NAMED *CITY'S* YOUNG PLAYER OF THE YEAR THE FOLLOWING YEAR. HE JOINED *BARCELONA*, WAS LOANED OUT TO *SEVILLA*, SOLD TO *VILLARREAL*, BOUGHT BACK BY *BARCELONA*, WHO LOANED HIM OUT TO *ARSENAL* BEFORE SELLING HIM TO *CELTA VIGA*.

**4** *CITY* MANAGER WHO PLAYED FOR *MANCHESTER UNITED, BARCELONA, BAYERN MUNICH, CHELSEA, SOUTHAMPTON, EVERTON* AND *BLACKBURN ROVERS*.

**5** CAPPED 22 TIMES BY SPAIN, HE WON MULTIPLE HONOURS WITH *BARCELONA*, INCLUDING FOUR LEAGUE TITLES, THE EUROPEAN CUP AND THE UEFA CUP WINNERS' CUP, AND WAS APPOINTED DIRECTOR OF FOOTBALL AT *CITY* IN 2012.

**6** *SPAIN* WINGER WHOSE PREVIOUS CLUBS INCLUDED *BARCELONA*, *BENFICA* AND *CELTA VIGO*, HE SPENT JUST ONE UNSETTLED SEASON IN MANCHESTER IN 2016-17 BEFORE JOINING *SEVILLA*.

**7**   *BRAZIL* INTERNATIONAL FULL-BACK, FORMERLY OF *ARSENAL*, HE WAS SIGNED BY *CITY* FROM *BARCELONA* IN 2009.

**8**   FORMER *BARCELONA* VICE-PRESIDENT, CEO OF *MANCHESTER CITY*, *NEW YORK CITY FC* AND *MELBOURNE CITY FC*.

**9**   HE BEGAN HIS CAREER AT *BARCELONA* AND PLAYED FOR *PARIS SAINT-GERMAIN*, *RANGERS*, *REAL SOCIEDAD*, *EVERTON* AND *ARSENAL* BEFORE BECOMING ASSISTANT COACH AT *CITY*.

**10**   BETWEEN MANAGING *BARCELONA* AND *BAYERN MUNICH*, *CITY* MANAGER *PEP GUARDIOLA* TOOK A ONE-YEAR SABBATICAL IN WHICH CITY?

# MOLINEUX-BIES

**KEITH CURLE** EXPERIENCED PROMOTION WITH **BRISTOL CITY** AND RELEGATION WITH **READING** BEFORE SPENDING A COUPLE OF YEARS WITH **WIMBLEDON'S "CRAZY GANG"**. HE JOINED **CITY** IN 1991 FOR A CLUB RECORD £2.5 MILLION AND IN FIVE YEARS IN MANCHESTER, WAS MADE CLUB CAPTAIN AND EARNED HIS FIRST **ENGLAND** CAPS. FOLLOWING THE DISMISSAL OF MANAGER **PETER REID**, **CURLE** WAS STRIPPED OF THE **CITY** CAPTAINCY AND SOLD TO **WOLVERHAMPTON WANDERERS**.

IDENTIFY THESE OTHER **CITY** PLAYERS WHO ALSO PLAYED FOR **WOLVES**.

**1** HE WAS TOP SCORER FOR **WOLVES** IN THE TITLE-WINNING 1957-58 SEASON AND WON AN FA CUP IN 1960 BEFORE JOINING **CITY** IN 1963. HE WON PROMOTION WITH **CITY** IN 1966 BEFORE LEAVING FOR **WALSALL**.

**2** SCOTTISH LEFT-BACK SIGNED TO **CITY** FROM **COVENTRY CITY** IN 1980, HE PLAYED IN THE 1981 FA CUP FINAL BEFORE WINNING TWO PROMOTIONS WITH **OXFORD UNITED** AND PLAYING FOR **LEEDS UNITED** AND **WOLVES**.

**3** NICKNAMED **"WAGGY"**, HE WAS A FLYING WINGER FOR **CITY** WHO BECAME A CLUB LEGEND WITH **WOLVERHAMPTON WANDERERS**, MAKING 404 APPEARANCES IN 12 YEARS BEFORE MOVING ON TO **BLACKBURN ROVERS** -- WHERE HE BECAME THE FIRST PLAYER IN ENGLISH FOOTBALL TO RECEIVE A RED CARD!

**4** DURING LOANS FROM **CITY** IN 1986-87, HE KEPT GOAL FOR FOUR CLUBS IN FOUR DIVISIONS OVER 9 WEEKS, PLAYING WITH FOURTH DIVISION **WOLVES**, THIRD DIVISION **CARLISLE UNITED**, SECOND DIVISION **BRADFORD CITY** AND FIRST DIVISION **SOUTHAMPTON!**

**5** HIS £1,437,500 TRANSFER WAS NAMED THE NUMBER ONE BIGGEST WASTE OF MONEY IN FOOTBALL HISTORY BY **THE GUARDIAN**.

**6** WINGER WHO CAME THROUGH THE RANKS AT **CITY** BEFORE LENGTHY SPELLS WITH **OXFORD UNITED**, **DERBY COUNTY** AND **WOLVES**. AN **ENGLAND U-21** INTERNATIONAL, HE MANAGED THE TEAM THAT WON THE FIFA UNDER-20S WORLD CUP IN SOUTH KOREA IN 2017.

**7**  LAUNCHED HIS CAREER WITH **BLACKPOOL**, SPENT A LITTLE OVER A YEAR WITH **CITY**, WON THE 1991 FA CUP WITH **SPURS** BEFORE AN UNHAPPY TIME WITH L**IVERPOOL** SAW HIM LOANED OUT TO FOUR CLUBS, INCLUDING **WOLVERHAMPTON WANDERERS**.

**8**  NICKNAMED "**THE KANGAROO KID**" FOR HIS JUMPING ABILITY, HE WON A 1960 FA CUP MEDAL WITH **WOLVES** BEFORE JOINING **CITY** IN 1964, BUT MOVED ON TO **ASTON VILLA** THE SAME YEAR.

**9**  GOALKEEPER NICKNAMED "**BUDGIE**".

**10**  PLAYER OF THE YEAR AT **WOLVERHAMPTON WANDERERS** AND **EVERTON**, HE JOINED **CITY** IN 2009, GOING ON TO WIN TWO LEAGUE TITLES, THE FA CUP AND THE LEAGUE CUP BEFORE DEPARTING FOR **WEST BROMWICH ALBION** FIVE YEARS LATER.

# BLED BLUE BLOOD

SON OF A POLICEMAN, TWO-TIME *CITY* PLAYER OF THE YEAR *MIKE DOYLE* WAS A HARD-AS-NAILS MIDFIELDER WHOSE PASSION FOR *CITY* WAS ONLY MATCHED BY HIS LOATHING OF *MANCHESTER UNITED*. SIGNED FROM *STOCKPORT BOYS* IN 1962, HE BROKE INTO THE SENIOR TEAM IN 1965, AND WENT ON TO MAKE 570 APPEARANCES FOR *CITY*. HIS LATER YEARS WERE MARRED BY A STRUGGLE WITH ALCOHOLISM AND HE DIED OF LIVER FAILURE IN 2011 AT THE AGE OF 64.

**1** WHAT WAS *MIKE DOYLE'S* NICKNAME IN HIS *CITY* DAYS?

**2** WHO WAS THE LEGENDARY CHIEF SCOUT WHO DISCOVERED *DOYLE*, AS WELL AS SUCH OTHER CITY TALENT AS *ALAN OAKES, STAN BOWLES, JOE CORRIGAN, WILLIE DONACHIE, TOMMY BOOTH, TONY TOWERS, PAUL POWER* AND *GLYN PARDOE?*

**3** WHICH C*ITY* MANAGER MADE *DOYLE* CAPTAIN IN 1975?

**4** *DOYLE* CAPTAINED THE 1976 LEAGUE CUP-WINNING SIDE, THE LAST *CITY* CAPTAIN TO LIFT A TROPHY UNTIL WHICH PLAYER?

**5** HOW MANY TIMES WAS *DOYLE* CAPPED BY *ENGLAND?*
A) FIVE   B) TEN   C) FIFTEEN

**6** *MALCOLM ALLISON* DROPPED *DOYLE* FROM THE *CITY* SIDE IN 1972 TO ACCOMMODATE WHICH PLAYER, UNBALANCING A TEAM THAT HAD SEEMED DESTINED FOR ANOTHER LEAGUE TITLE?

**7** AFTER LEAVING MANCHESTER *CITY* IN 1978, HE SPENT THREE AND A HALF YEARS AT WHICH CLUB, HELPING THEM WIN PROMOTION TO THE TOP FLIGHT IN 1979?

**8** HE MOVED ON TO WHICH CLUB IN JANUARY, 1982?

**9** *DOYLE* ENDED HIS PLAYING CAREER AFTER MAKING 24 APPEARANCES IN THE OLD FOURTH DIVISION FOR WHICH NORTH-WEST CLUB?

**10** HIS GRANDSON, *TOMMY DOYLE*, IS ALSO THE GRANDSON OF WHICH OTHER *CITY* GREAT?

# CRÈME DE LA PREM

PLAYING 653 GAMES FOR **ASTON VILLA**, **CITY**, **EVERTON** AND **WEST BROMWICH ALBION** OVER 23 SEASONS, **GARETH BARRY** SET THE RECORD FOR THE HIGHEST NUMBER OF PREMIER LEAGUE APPEARANCES.

IDENTIFY THESE OTHER RECORD-SETTERS WHO HAVE PLAYED FOR **CITY**:

**1** OLDEST PREMIER LEAGUE PLAYER, AGED 43 YEARS AND 162 DAYS, **CITY** V **CRYSTAL PALACE**, 1995

**2** MOST GOALS IN A 42-GAME PREMIER LEAGUE SEASON, PLAYING FOR **NEWCASTLE UNITED**, 1993-94

**3** HOW MANY GAMES DID IT TAKE **PEP GUARDIOLA** TO RECORD 100 WINS IN RECORD TIME?

**4** WHO HOLDS THE RECORD FOR MOST PREMIER LEAGUE OWN GOALS, PUTTING THROUGH HIS OWN GOAL ON 10 OCCASIONS?

**5** **SERGIO AGÜERO** SHARES THE RECORD FOR MOST GOALS IN A PREMIER LEAGUE GAME, SCORING FIVE AGAINST **NEWCASTLE UNITED** IN 2015. NAME THE FOUR PLAYERS -- ONE OF WHOM LATER PLAYED FOR **CITY** -- WITH WHOM HE SHARES THAT RECORD.

**6** **KEVIN DE BRUYNE** SHARES THE RECORD OF 20 PREMIER LEAGUE ASSISTS IN A SEASON WITH WHICH ARSENAL **PLAYER?**

**7** SENT OFF EIGHT TIMES, WHICH TWO **CITY** PLAYERS SHARE THE RECORD FOR MOST DISMISSALS WITH **DUNCAN FERGUSON?**

**8** WHO SHARES THE RECORD OF FOUR PREMIER LEAGUE GOLDEN GLOVES WITH **PETR ČECH?**

**9** **SERGIO AGÜERO** AND **THIERRY HENRY** SHARE THE RECORD FOR THE MOST CONSECUTIVE SEASONS SCORING 20 GOALS -- HOW MANY SEASONS?

**10** WHO HOLDS THE RECORD FOR SCORING FOR THE LARGEST NUMBER OF PREMIER LEAGUE TEAMS?

# THRASHINGS!

THE FIRST GOALKEEPER TO CAPTAIN *ENGLAND* SINCE THE 19TH CENTURY, *FRANK SWIFT* WAS BORN IN BLACKPOOL, ON BOXING DAY, 1914. HE MADE HIS SENIOR DEBUT FOR *MANCHESTER CITY* ON CHRISTMAS DAY, 1933, THE DAY BEFORE HIS 19TH BIRTHDAY. *CITY* WENT ON TO WIN THE FA CUP THAT SEASON, AND *"BIG FRANK"* FAINTED ON HIS WAY UP TO RECEIVE HIS WINNER'S MEDAL! THREE YEARS LATER, HE WON A LEAGUE CHAMPIONSHIP WITH *CITY*. THE SECOND WORLD WAR INTERRUPTED HIS PLAYING CAREER ... AND WHEN FOOTBALL RESUMED, HE WAS A MEMBER OF THE TEAM THAT ENDURED *CITY'S* HEAVIEST FA CUP DEFEAT OF THE 20TH CENTURY, AN 8-2 THRASHING AT THE HANDS OF *BRADFORD PARK AVENUE.*

IDENTIFY THE OPPONENTS IN THESE OTHER RECORD-SETTING GAMES:

**1** RECORD LEAGUE VICTORY (GOALS SCORED): 11-3, MARCH 1895

**2** RECORD LEAGUE DEFEAT (GOALS CONCEDED): 2-10, MARCH 1893

**3** RECORD PREMIER LEAGUE VICTORY: 8-0, SEPTEMBER 2019

**4** RECORD PREMIER LEAGUE DEFEAT: 1-8, MAY 2008

**5** RECORD FA CUP VICTORY: 12-0, OCTOBER 1890

**6** RECORD FA CUP DEFEAT (GOALS CONCEDED): 2-8, JANUARY 1946

**7** RECORD LEAGUE CUP VICTORY: 9-0, JANUARY 2019

**8** RECORD LEAGUE CUP DEFEAT: 0-4, OCTOBER 1995

**9** RECORD EUROPEAN VICTORY: 7-0, MARCH 2019

**10** RECORD EUROPEAN DEFEAT: 0-4, OCTOBER 2016

# "UNCLE JOE" MERCER

AS MANAGER, *JOE MERCER* STEERED *CITY* TO THE SECOND DIVISION TITLE, THE FIRST DIVISION CHAMPIONSHIP, THE FA CUP, THE LEAGUE CUP, AND THE EUROPEAN CUP WINNERS' CUP.

**1**   AS A PLAYER, *MERCER* WON HIS FIRST LEAGUE TITLE IN 1939 PLAYING FOR WHICH NORTH WEST CLUB?

**2**   FOLLOWING THE SECOND WORLD WAR, HE WON TWO LEAGUE TITLES AND AN FA CUP WITH WHICH CLUB?

**3**   NAME ONE OF THE TWO CLUBS THAT *JOE MERCER* MANAGED BEFORE TAKING OVER AT *MANCHESTER CITY* IN 1965.

**4**   WHO DID HE SUCCEED AS *MANCHESTER CITY* MANAGER?

**5**   WHO WAS THE CLUB CHAIRMAN WHO HIRED HIM AS *CITY* BOSS?

**6**   FOLLOWING THE TAKEOVER WRANGLINGS AT *MANCHESTER CITY* THAT EVENTUALLY SAW *PETER SWALES* INSTALLED AS CHAIRMAN, *JOE MERCER* WAS APPOINTED MANAGER OF WHICH CLUB?

**7**   BORN IN 1914, *MERCER* WAS A NATIVE OF ELLESMERE PORT, CHESHIRE, AS WERE TWO OF THE PLAYERS IN HIS *CITY* SIDE THAT WON THE 1969 FA CUP. ONE WAS A LEFT WINGER WHO LATER WON A FOURTH DIVISION TITLE WITH *DONCASTER ROVERS*, PLAYED IN SOUTH AFRICA AND EVENTUALLY EMIGRATED TO AUSTRALIA, THE OTHER WENT ON TO WIN A LEAGUE TITLE AND TWO EUROPEAN CUPS WITH *NOTTINGHAM FOREST*. CAN YOU NAME EITHER PLAYER?

**8**   IN 1974, *MERCER* WAS APPOINTED CARETAKER MANAGER OF *ENGLAND* FOLLOWING THE DEPARTURE OF WHICH MANAGER?

**9**   WHICH TV PRESENTER SURPRISED *JOE MERCER* WHEN THE *MANCHESTER CITY* BOSS WAS THE SUBJECT OF TELEVISION'S *"THIS IS YOUR LIFE"* PROGRAMME IN MARCH, 1970?

**10**   *MERCER* DIED IN 1990, THE SAME YEAR AS WHICH *CITY* GREAT AND LONG-TIME MANAGER OF *NORTHERN IRELAND?*

# "THE HONEY MONSTER"

BORN IN TALLAGHT, DUBLIN, IN 1979, *RICHARD DUNNE* JOINED *EVERTON* AS A 15-YEAR-OLD SCHOOLBOY. HE WAS PART OF THE CLUB'S SUCCESSFUL 1998 FA YOUTH SQUAD, ALONG WITH *LEON OSMAN* AND *TONY HIBBERT*. AFTER JOINING *CITY* IN A £3.5 MILLION TRANSFER DEAL IN 2000 THAT SAW HIM RELEGATED IN HIS DEBUT SEASON, HE HELPED SECURE PROMOTION IN 2002. NICKNAMED *"THE HONEY MONSTER"*, IN HIS TEN SEASONS AT THE CLUB, HE WAS VOTED *CITY* PLAYER OF THE YEAR FOUR TIMES.  CAPPED 80 TIMES BY *REPUBLIC OF IRELAND*, HE RETIRED IN 2015, MOVING WITH HIS FAMILY TO MONTE CARLO.

**1** WHICH MANAGER DID HE PLAY UNDER AT *EVERTON* AND *CITY?*

**2** ALTHOUGH HE BECAME ONE OF *CITY'S* BEST CENTRAL DEFENDERS, HE WAS ORIGINALLY SIGNED AS ONE OF TWO REPLACEMENTS FOR RIGHT-BACK *RICHARD EDGHILL*, ALONG WITH WHICH FRENCH DEFENDER SIGNED FROM *NEWCASTLE UNITED?*

**3** WHICH *CITY* EXECUTIVE WAS QUOTED AS SAYING: *"CHINA AND INDIA ARE GAGGING FOR FOOTBALL CONTENT TO WATCH AND WE'RE GOING TO TELL THEM THAT CITY IS THEIR CONTENT. WE NEED A SUPERSTAR TO GET THROUGH THAT DOOR. RICHARD DUNNE DOESN'T ROLL OFF THE TONGUE IN BEIJING".*

**4** HE LEFT *CITY* TO JOIN WHICH CLUB IN 2009?

**5** WHO WAS THE MANAGER, A FORMER *CITY* AND *NORTHERN IRELAND* MIDFIELDER, WHO SIGNED *DUNNE* TO THAT CLUB?

**6** *DUNNE* WAS ON THE LOSING SIDE IN THE 2010 LEAGUE CUP FINAL -- WHO WERE THE OPPONENTS?

**7** HE SIGNED FOR WHICH CLUB ON A FREE TRANSFER IN 2013, EXPERIENCING PROMOTION AND RELEGATION IN THE TWO SEASONS HE PLAYED BEFORE RETIRING?

**8** IN **DUNNE'S** FINAL SEASON, WHICH FORMER **CITY** PLAYER WAS BRIEFLY APPOINTED JOINT CARETAKER MANAGER OF THAT CLUB AFTER THE DEPARTURE OF **HARRY REDKNAPP?**

**9** WHICH FORMER **CITY** PLAYER WAS THE MANAGER WHO GAVE **DUNNE** HIS FIRST **REPUBLIC OF IRELAND** CAP IN 2000?

**10** WHICH FORMER **CITY** PLAYER GAVE **DUNNE** HIS 60TH AND FINAL **REPUBLIC OF IRELAND** CAP IN 2013?

# THE DERBY

SINCE **ST. MARK'S (WEST GORTON)** -- THE CLUB THAT WOULD SOON MORPH INTO **MANCHESTER CITY** -- LOST 3-0 TO **MANCHESTER UNITED** PRECURSORS **NEWTON HEATH** IN 1881, DERBY GAMES HAVE THROWN UP DRAMA, INTRIGUE AND SEISMIC SHIFTS IN THE BALANCE OF POWER. ONE OF THE MOST ICONIC MOMENTS IN RECENT YEARS CAME AT **OLD TRAFFORD** IN 2011, WHEN THE MERCURIAL **MARIO BALOTELLI** OPENED THE SCORING IN **CITY'S** 6-1 DEMOLITION OF **UNITED** AND REVEALED HIS INFAMOUS **"WHY ALWAYS ME?"** T-SHIRT CELEBRATION.

**1**  IN THAT 6-1 **CITY** WIN IN 2011, WHO WAS THE **UNITED** PLAYER RED-CARDED IN THE 47TH MINUTE FOR A FOUL ON **BALOTELLI?**

**2**  IN 1970, **CITY** FULL-BACK **GLYN PARDOE'S** LEG WAS BROKEN IN TWO PLACES FOLLOWING A TACKLE BY WHICH **UNITED** PLAYER?

**3**  IN THE 1974 **MAINE ROAD** DERBY, WHICH **CITY** PLAYER WAS DISMISSED ALONG WITH **UNITED'S LOU MACARI**, BOTH REFUSING TO LEAVE THE PITCH? REFEREE **CLIVE THOMAS** SENT BOTH TEAMS TO THE DRESSING ROOMS AND INSISTED POLICE NOT ALLOW THE TWO PLAYERS TO RETURN WHEN THE GAME WAS RESTARTED.

**4**  **UNITED'S ROY KEANE** WAS HEAVILY FINED AND SUSPENDED FOLLOWING HIS PREMEDITATED REVENGE TACKLE ON WHICH **CITY** PLAYER IN 2001?

**5**  WHICH **UNITED** PLAYER WAS SENT OFF FOR HEADBUTTING **SERGIO AGÜERO** IN 2017?

**6**  A TACKLE BY **UNITED'S MARTIN BUCHAN** IN A 1975 DERBY GAME RESULTED IN THE SERIOUS INJURY THAT EFFECTIVELY ENDED THE TOP FLIGHT CAREER OF WHICH **CITY** AND **ENGLAND** STAR?

**7**  WHICH **UNITED** PLAYER WAS RED CARDED IN DERBY GAMES IN BOTH 2006 AND 2008?

**8** IN 2004, WHICH *UNITED* PLAYER WAS BOOKED FOR DIVING AND THEN SENT OFF AFTER BUTTING *CITY'S STEVE MCMANAMAN?*

**9** WHICH PLAYER, WHO WAS ON THE BOOKS OF BOTH CLUBS, SCORED FIVE TIMES FOR *UNITED* AND THREE TIMES FOR *CITY* IN DERBIES?

**10** IN A 2012 DERBY GAME IN THE THIRD ROUND OF THE FA CUP, WHICH *CITY* PLAYER WAS SENT OFF FOR A FOUL ON *NANI?*

# A MAN IN A MILLION

IN 1979, **TREVOR FRANCIS** BECAME THE FIRST MILLION POUND FOOTBALLER WITH HIS TRANSFER FROM **BIRMINGHAM CITY** TO **NOTTINGHAM FOREST**. HE WON THE EUROPEAN CUP TWICE UNDER **BRIAN CLOUGH**, SCORING THE ONLY GOAL OF THE GAME IN THE FIRST FINAL, BUT MISSING THE SECOND THROUGH AN ACHILLES INJURY THAT ALSO RULED HIM OUT OF THE **ENGLAND** TEAM THAT WENT TO THE 1980 EUROPEAN CHAMPIONSHIP. HE JOINED **CITY** IN 1981 BUT FAILED TO JUSTIFY THE £1.2 MILLION FEE AS HE WAS FREQUENTLY INJURED THROUGHOUT THE ONE SEASON HE SPENT AT **MAINE ROAD.**

**1** WHO WAS THE MANAGER WHO SIGNED **FRANCIS** TO **CITY?**

**2** HE SCORED TWICE FOR **ENGLAND** AT THE 1982 WORLD CUP -- AGAINST WHICH TWO TEAMS?

**3** HE HAD SPENT TIME PLAYING IN THE NASL FOR **DETROIT EXPRESS**, A TEAM CO-OWNED BY WHICH TV PUNDIT AND CHAIRMAN OF **COVENTRY CITY?**

**4** HE WAS TRANSFERRED TO WHICH ITALIAN CLUB IN 1982?

**5** HE MOVED TO WHICH OTHER ITALIAN CLUB IN 1986?

**6** HE PLAYED ALONGSIDE GRAEME SOUNESS IN ITALY AND RETURNED TO BRITAIN IN 1987 TO PLAY UNDER HIM AT WHICH CLUB?

**7** HE SIGNED FOR WHICH TEAM IN 1988, TAKING OVER AS PLAYER-MANAGER LATER THAT YEAR WHEN **JIM SMITH** LEFT FOR **NEWCASTLE UNITED?**

**8** HE ENDED HIS PLAYING DAYS AT WHICH YORKSHIRE CLUB, TAKING OVER AS MANAGER FOLLOWING **RON ATKINSON'S** DEPARTURE?

**9** HE SPENT FIVE YEARS, FROM 1996 TO 2001, AS MANAGER OF WHICH CLUB, TAKING THEM TO THE 2001 LEAGUE CUP FINAL?

**10** HIS LAST JOB IN MANAGEMENT WAS AT THE HELM OF WHICH LONDON CLUB BETWEEN 2001 AND 2003?

# BUZZER!

MIKE SUMMERBEE MADE HIS DEBUT FOR SWINDON TOWN AT THE AGE OF 16 AND PLAYED MORE THAN 200 TIMES FOR THE WILTSHIRE CLUB OVER THE NEXT SIX YEARS. JOE MERCER HAD PLAYED WITH MIKE'S DAD DURING THE WAR AND SIGNED FLYING WINGER MIKE PRIOR TO THE 1965-66 SEASON. IT WAS A SMART PIECE OF BUSINESS, "BUZZER" HELPING THE CLUB TO PROMOTION TO THE TOP FLIGHT IN HIS DEBUT SEASON BEFORE GOING ON TO BECOME A GENUINE CITY LEGEND.

**1** MIKE SCORED THE OPENING GOAL IN THE 4-3 VICTORY AWAY TO NEWCASTLE UNITED ON THE FINAL DAY OF THE SEASON THAT SECURED THE TITLE IN 1968 -- WHO SCORED CITY'S OTHER THREE GOALS THAT DAY?

**2** MIKE WAS ONCE PARTNERS IN A FASHION BOUTIQUE WITH WHICH MANCHESTER UNITED STAR?

**3** SUMMERBEE WAS SUBSTITUTED IN THE 1970 LEAGUE CUP FINAL WIN OVER WEST BROMWICH ALBION AT WEMBLEY AFTER SUSTAINING A HAIRLINE FRACTURE OF THE LEG. WEST BROM WERE HAMPERED WHEN INJURY ENFORCED THE SUBSTITUTION OF WHICH MIDFIELDER, WHO WOULD SUBSEQUENTLY BE ON THE WINNING SIDE WHEN CITY WON THE LEAGUE CUP AGAIN IN 1976?

**4** MIKE JOINED WHICH CLUB IN 1975?

**5** 18 MONTHS LATER, HE MOVED TO WHICH OTHER NORTH WEST CLUB?

**6** SUMMERBEE ENDED HIS LEAGUE CAREER AS PLAYER-MANAGER OF WHICH CLUB?

**7** MIKE APPEARED IN THE 1981 MOVIE "ESCAPE TO VICTORY", ALONGSIDE MICHAEL CAINE, SYLVESTER STALLONE AND A NUMBER OF FOOTBALLERS, INCLUDING BOBBY MOORE AND PELÉ. WHAT WAS MIKE'S CHARACTER CALLED?

**8** MIKE'S SON ALSO PLAYED FOR SWINDON TOWN AND CITY -- WHAT IS HIS NAME?

**9** HOW MANY *ENGLAND* CAPS DID *MIKE SUMMERBEE* WIN?
A) FIVE   B) EIGHT   C) TWELVE

**10** FOLLOWING THE TAKEOVER BY THE *ABU DHABI UNITED GROUP,*
WHAT OFFICIAL ROLE DID *MIKE SUMMERBEE* TAKE WITH *CITY?*

# TRAVELLING THE EAST LANCS ROAD

A PRODUCT OF THE **LEEDS UNITED** ACADEMY, **JAMES MILNER** MADE HIS PREMIER LEAGUE DEBUT AT THE AGE OF 16 YEARS AND 309 DAYS, AND BECAME THE YOUNGEST PREMIER LEAGUE SCORER A FEW DAYS BEFORE HIS 17TH BIRTHDAY. HIS CAREER TOOK HIM TO **SWINDON TOWN**, **NEWCASTLE UNITED** AND **ASTON VILLA**, BEFORE HE SIGNED FOR **CITY** IN 2010. HE WON MULTIPLE HONOURS, INCLUDING TWO LEAGUE TITLES, THE FA CUP AND THE LEAGUE CUP, BEFORE JOINING **LIVERPOOL** IN 2015. HIS **ANFIELD** TROPHY HAUL HAS INCLUDED THE PREMIER LEAGUE AND THE UEFA CHAMPIONS LEAGUE.

IDENTIFY THESE **CITY** PLAYERS WHO ALSO PLAYED FOR **LIVERPOOL**:

**1** BETWEEN LEAVING **LIVERPOOL** AND JOINING **CITY** IN 2003, HE WON TWO UEFA CHAMPIONS LEAGUES WITH **REAL MADRID**.

**2** PLAYED UNDER HIS FATHER AT **NOTTINGHAM FOREST**, WITH WHOM HE WON TWO LEAGUE CUPS, HIS MANAGEMENT CAREER HAS TAKEN HIM FROM **BURTON ALBION** TO **MANSFIELD TOWN**.

**3** VETERAN GOALKEEPER WHO MADE ONE APPEARANCE FOR **CITY'S** 2020-21 TITLE WINNING TEAM.

**4** STRIKER WHOSE CV INCLUDES **CHARLTON ATHLETIC**, **LUTON TOWN**, **LIVERPOOL**, **TOTTENHAM HOTSPUR** AND **QUEENS PARK RANGERS**, HE PLAYED FOR **CITY** IN THE MID-1990S IN BETWEEN TWO SPELLS WITH **PORTSMOUTH**.

**5** **IVORY COAST** DEFENDER WHO WON LEAGUE TITLES WITH **ARSENAL**, **CITY** AND **CELTIC**.

**6** WON MULTIPLE HONOURS WITH **LIVERPOOL** BEFORE JOINING **CITY** IN 1991 AND LATER MANAGED **SWINDON TOWN** AND **BLACKPOOL**.

**7** 1934 FA CUP WINNER WITH **CITY**, HE CAPTAINED **LIVERPOOL** BEFORE MOVING INTO MANAGEMENT AFTER THE SECOND WORLD WAR AND SUBSEQUENTLY WINNING THE EUROPEAN CUP.

**8**   **ENGLAND** STAR WHOSE CLUBS INCLUDED **NEWCASTLE UNITED,** **CITY, EVERTON, BOLTON** AND **FULHAM,** BUT WHOSE ONLY HONOURS WERE WON WITH **LIVERPOOL** FOLLOWING HIS RECORD TRANSFER IN 1987.

**9**   HIS 1987 TRANSFER TO **CITY** EARNED A CLUB RECORD FEE FOR **BLACKPOOL,** HE WON THE 1991 FA CUP WITH **SPURS,** BUT SUBSEQUENTLY STRUGGLED AT **LIVERPOOL.**

**10**   STRIKER CAPPED EIGHT TIMES BY **ENGLAND,** HIS **LIVERPOOL** TROPHY HAUL INCLUDES FOUR LEAGUE TITLES AND THREE EUROPEAN CUPS AND HE WAS INDUCTED INTO THE **IPSWICH TOWN** HALL OF FAME.

# GOING FOR GOLD

THE DAY BEFORE THE 2016 OLYMPICS COMMENCED, IT WAS CONFIRMED THAT *PALMEIRAS* PRODIGY *GABRIEL JESUS* WOULD BE JOINING *CITY.* OVER THE NEXT FEW WEEKS, THE £27 MILLION FEE LOOKED TO BE MONEY WELL SPENT, AS *JESUS* HELPED HIS COUNTRY WIN OLYMPIC GOLD.

IDENTIFY THESE OTHER OLYMPIC MEDAL-WINNING *MANCHESTER CITY* STARS:

**1**  TOP SCORER WITH 9 GOALS AT THE 1972 OLYMPICS, INCLUDING BOTH GOALS IN *POLAND'S* 2-1 FINAL VICTORY OVER *HUNGARY*.

**2**  *PEP GUARDIOLA* WON GOLD AT THE 1992 OLYMPICS WHEN *SPAIN* BEAT WHICH NATION 3-2 IN THE FINAL?

**3**  MIDFIELDER WHO JOINED *CITY* ON LOAN FROM *ROMA* IN 2012, HE WON AN OLYMPIC BRONZE MEDAL WITH *CHILE* IN 2000.

**4**  TOP SCORER AT THE 2004 TOURNAMENT, HE WON A GOLD MEDAL AS *ARGENTINA* BEAT *PARAGUAY* 1-0 IN THE FINAL.

**5**  SCORED TWICE FOR *ARGENTINA* IN THE 2008 TOURNAMENT SEMI-FINAL BEFORE GOING ON TO CAPTURE OLYMPIC GOLD.

**6**  THREE DAYS AFTER WINNING OLYMPIC GOLD WITH *ARGENTINA* IN 2008, HE SIGNED TO *CITY* FROM *ESPANYOL*.

**7**  WEEKS AFTER SIGNING TO *CITY* FROM *CSKA MOSCOW* IN 2008, HE WON BRONZE WITH *BRAZIL*, SCORING TWO GOALS IN THE TOURNAMENT.

# GOING UP!

THE 23 GOALS SCORED BY LOCAL LAD *JOE ROYLE* WERE INSTRUMENTAL IN PROPELLING *EVERTON* TO THE LEAGUE TITLE IN 1970. HE WON THE LEAGUE CUP WITH *CITY* IN 1976, AND PLAYED FOR *BRISTOL CITY* AND *NORWICH CITY* BEFORE LAUNCHING HIS MANAGEMENT CAREER AT *OLDHAM ATHLETIC*. HE STEERED *"THE LATICS"* TO PROMOTION AND WON THE FA CUP WITH *EVERTON*, BEFORE TAKING THE REINS AT *CITY* IN FEBRUARY, 1998. HIS ARRIVAL WAS NOT ENOUGH TO HALT THE SLIDE INTO THE THIRD TIER, BUT HE TURNED THE CLUB'S FORTUNES AROUND, DELIVERING CONSECUTIVE PROMOTIONS IN THE NEXT TWO SEASONS. UNFORTUNATELY, *CITY'S* STAY IN THE PREMIER LEAGUE WAS BRIEF AND THEY WERE IMMEDIATELY RELEGATED, ENDING *ROYLE'S* REIGN.

WHO WERE THE MANAGERS WHO DELIVERED THESE PROMOTIONS?

**1**    1895-96, SECOND DIVISION RUNNERS-UP (SECOND TIER)

**2**    1898-99, SECOND DIVISION CHAMPIONS (SECOND TIER)

**3**    1902-03, SECOND DIVISION CHAMPIONS (SECOND TIER)

**4**    1909-10, SECOND DIVISION CHAMPIONS (SECOND TIER)

**5**    1927-28, SECOND DIVISION CHAMPIONS (SECOND TIER)

**6**    1946-47, SECOND DIVISION CHAMPIONS (SECOND TIER)

**7**    1950-51, SECOND DIVISION RUNNERS-UP (SECOND TIER)

**8**    1965-66, SECOND DIVISION CHAMPIONS (SECOND TIER)

**9**    1984-85, PROMOTED, 3RD PLACE, SECOND DIVISION (SECOND TIER)

**10**    1988-89, SECOND DIVISION RUNNERS-UP (SECOND TIER)

**11**    2001-02, FIRST DIVISION CHAMPIONS (SECOND TIER)

# CITY'S AFRICANS

A 2004 AFRICA CUP OF NATIONS WINNER WITH *TUNISIA*, *HATEM TRABELSI* REPRESENTED HIS COUNTRY AT THREE WORLD CUPS. HE WON LEAGUE AND CUP HONOURS WITH *AJAX* BEFORE JOINING *CITY* IN 2006.

WHICH AFRICAN COUNTRY CAPPED THE FOLLOWING *CITY* PLAYERS?

**1**   *RIYAD MAHREZ*

**2**   *WILFRIED BONY*

**3**   *MARC-VIVIEN FOÉ*

**4**   *ALEX NIMELY*

**5**   *KOLO TOURÉ*

**6**   *KELECHI IHEANACHO*

**7**   *EMMANUEL ADEBAYOR*

**8**   *ALI BENARBIA*

**9**   *BENJANI*

**10**  *GEORGE WEAH*

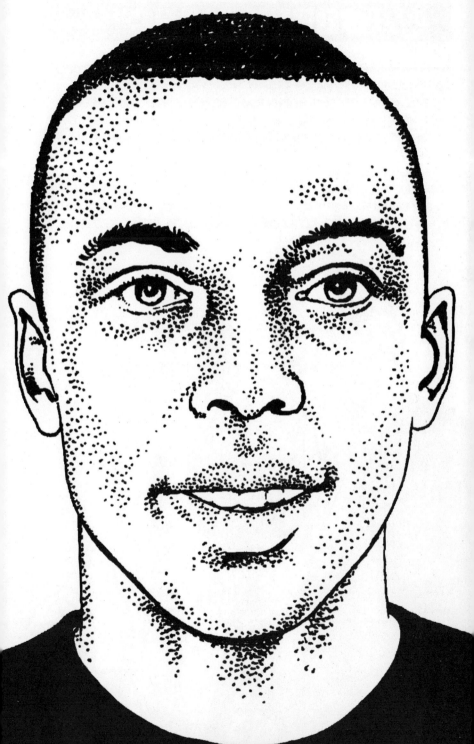

# "BOBBY MANC"

IN HIS FIRST SEASON AT THE HELM, *ROBERTO MANCINI* STEERED *CITY* TO THE CLUB'S FIRST MAJOR TROPHY IN 35 YEARS, THE 2011 FA CUP. THE FOLLOWING SEASON, HE INSCRIBED HIS NAME INTO *CITY* LEGEND WHEN HE DELIVERED THE PREMIER LEAGUE, ENDING A 44-YEAR WAIT TO BE THE TOP CLUB IN ENGLISH FOOTBALL ONCE MORE. SACKED TWO DAYS AFTER *CITY'S* DEFEAT IN THE 2013 FA CUP FINAL, *MANCINI* -- WHO WAS AFFECTIONATELY DUBBED *"BOBBY MANC"* BY THE *CITY* FAITHFUL -- TOOK OUT A FULL PAGE ADVERT IN THE *MANCHESTER EVENING NEWS* TO SAY FAREWELL AND THANK THE FANS, AN ACT THAT WAS RECIPROCATED IN THE *GAZZETTA DELLO SPORT* BY A GROUP OF *CITY* SUPPORTERS.

**1** AFTER LAUNCHING HIS PLAYING CAREER AT *BOLOGNA*, *MANCINI* WON NUMEROUS HONOURS, INCLUDING A SERIE A TITLE AND THE EUROPEAN CUP WINNERS' CUP, WITH WHICH ITALIAN CLUB?

**2** *MANCINI* WON THE INAUGURAL SERIE A PLAYER OF THE YEAR AWARD IN 1997. WHICH ERSTWHILE *MANCHESTER CITY* PLAYER WON THE AWARD IN 2015?

**3** IN 1997, HE FOLLOWED MANAGER *SVEN-GÖRAN ERIKSSON* TO WHICH ITALIAN TEAM, WHERE HIS SUBSEQUENT HONOURS INCLUDE ANOTHER SERIE A TITLE AND EUROPEAN CUP WINNERS' CUP?

**4** HE JOINED WHICH PREMIER LEAGUE CLUB ON LOAN IN EARLY 2001?

**5** HOW MANY TIMES WAS HE CAPPED BY *ITALY?* A) 36   B) 66   C) 96

**6** HIS FIRST COACHING JOBS WERE AT *FIORENTINA* AND *LAZIO*, *ROBERTO* WINNING THE COPPA ITALIA WITH BOTH, BEFORE HE WON THREE CONSECUTIVE SERIE A TITLES AS MANAGER OF WHICH CLUB?

**7** HE REPLACED WHICH *MANCHESTER CITY* MANAGER IN LATE 2009?

**8** HE SUCCEEDED *FATIH TERIM* AT WHICH CLUB, GOING ON TO WIN THE TURKISH CUP IN 2014?

**9** *ROBERTO* MANAGED WHICH RUSSIAN TEAM IN 2017-18?

**10** HE WAS APPOINTED MANAGER OF *ITALY* IN 2018 AFTER THE FAILURE OF WHICH MANAGER TO STEER THE NATIONAL TEAM TO THE 2018 WORLD CUP TOURNAMENT?

# THE SCANDINAVIANS

AFTER LAUNCHING HIS CAREER AT *TRELLEBORG*, *ANDREAS ISAKSSON* WAS STILL IN HIS TEENS WHEN HE SIGNED FOR *JUVENTUS* IN 1999. UNABLE TO DISPLACE *EDWIN VAN DER SAR*, HE RETURNED TO SWEDEN, WHERE HE WON TWO LEAGUE TITLES WITH *DJURGÅRDEN* AND EARNED THE FIRST OF HIS TEN SWEDISH GOALKEEPER OF THE YEAR AWARDS. SPELLS IN FRANCE WITH *RENNES* AND IN ENGLAND WITH *CITY* WERE FOLLOWED BY A MOVE TO *PSV EINDHOVEN* IN 2008. CAPPED 133 TIMES BY *SWEDEN*, HE RETIRED IN 2018 AFTER WINNING THE SWEDISH CUP WITH *DJURGÅRDEN*.

WHAT NATIONALITY ARE THE FOLLOWING SCANDINAVIAN *CITY* PLAYERS:

**1** *KASPER SCHMEICHEL*

**2** *RONNIE EKELUND*

**3** *AGE HAREIDE*

**4** *NICLAS JENSEN*

**5** *JOHN GUIDETTI*

**6** *KEVIN STUHR ELLEGAARD*

**7** *EGIL ØSTENSTAD*

**8** *MIKKEL BISCHOFF*

**9** *KÅRE INGEBRIGTSEN*

**10** *ALF-INGE HAALAND*

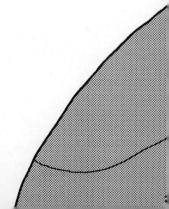

# THEM'S THE BREAKS

ALTHOUGH HE JOINED *CITY* FROM NON-LEAGUE *NELSON F.C.* IN 1951, *JACKIE DYSON* DIDN'T MAKE HIS SENIOR DEBUT UNTIL 1955, HIS PROGRESS HALTED BY HAVING TO COMPLETE HIS NATIONAL SERVICE. HE WAS AN IMMEDIATE SUCCESS IN THE FIRST TEAM, SCORING 13 TIMES IN 25 LEAGUE APPEARANCES IN THE SEASON THAT ENDED WITH THE 3-1 FA CUP FINAL WIN OVER *BIRMINGHAM*, A GAME IN WHICH HE SCORED *CITY'S* SECOND GOAL AND MADE THE THIRD FOR *BOBBY JOHNSTONE*. HIS CAREER WAS DERAILED BY TWO BROKEN LEGS IN A MATTER OF MONTHS THAT EFFECTIVELY ENDED HIS TOP FLIGHT CHANCES.

IDENTIFY THESE *CITY* PLAYERS BY THEIR BROKEN BONES:

**1** IN THE DAYS BEFORE SUBSTITUTES WERE ALLOWED, WHICH *CITY* GOALKEEPER, AFTER BREAKING A FINGER IN A GAME AGAINST *BURY*, WENT UP FRONT AND SCORED AN EQUALISING GOAL?

**2** WHILE ON INTERNATIONAL DUTY IN 2013, WHICH *CITY* STAR PLAYED 30 MINUTES AGAINST *SERBIA* WITH A BROKEN NOSE, MILD CONCUSSION AND A FRACTURED EYE SOCKET?

**3** WHICH SPANISH STRIKER FRACTURED THE FIFTH METATARSAL IN HIS RIGHT FOOT IN A 2014 PRE-SEASON FRIENDLY AGAINST SCOTTISH SIDE *HEARTS?*

**4** WHICH DEFENDER BROKE HIS LEG AND DISLOCATED HIS ANKLE PLAYING FOR *ATHLETIC BILBAO* IN MARCH, 2016, WHICH DELAYED HIS *CITY* TRANSFER UNTIL THE SUMMER OF 2018?

**5** WHICH 19-YEAR-OLD STRIKER SUFFERED A FRACTURED METATARSAL IN A GAME AGAINST *BOURNEMOUTH* JUST WEEKS AFTER JOINING *CITY* IN 2015?

**6** WHO SUSTAINED A FRACTURED NOSE AND EYE SOCKET DURING THE 2021 UEFA CHAMPIONS LEAGUE FINAL?

**7** WHICH *CITY* LEGEND SUSTAINED A HAIRLINE FRACTURE OF THE LEG IN THE 1970 LEAGUE CUP FINAL WIN AT WEMBLEY, RULING HIM OUT OF THE EUROPEAN CUP WINNERS' CUP FINAL SEVEN WEEKS LATER?

**8** WHICH *CITY* DEFENDER, CENTRE-HALF IN THE 1956 CUP FINAL THAT SAW *BERT TRAUTMANN* BREAK HIS NECK, BROKE HIS NOSE FIVE TIMES AND HIS ELBOW AND ANKLE ONCE DURING HIS TEN YEARS WITH THE CLUB?

# YOU KNOW MY NAME, LOOK UP MY NUMBER

WHEN **VINCENT KOMPANY** ARRIVED AT **CITY** FROM **HAMBURGER SV** IN 2008, HE TOOK THE NUMBER 33 SQUAD NUMBER. HE WAS HANDED THE NUMBER 4 JERSEY FOR THE 2010-11 SEASON AFTER PREVIOUS WEARER **NEDUM ONUOHA** MOVED ON LOAN TO **SUNDERLAND**.

**1** **FERRAN TORRES** INHERITED WHICH **DAVID SILVA** SHIRT NUMBER?

**2** **CITY** RETIRED THE NUMBER 23 SHIRT FOLLOWING THE SUDDEN DEATH OF WHICH CAMEROONIAN FORMER PLAYER?

**3** **FERNANDINHO** INHERITED THE 25 SHIRT NUMBER PREVIOUSLY WORN BY **JOE HART** AND WHICH AFRICAN PLAYER OF THE YEAR?

**4** HAVING PREVIOUSLY WORN NUMBER 16, **SERGIO AGÜERO** CLAIMED THE NUMBER 10 SHIRT FOLLOWING THE DEPARTURE OF WHICH STRIKER?

**5** WHICH SHIRT NUMBER LINKS **KEITH CURLE**, **PABLO ZABALETA** AND **JOHN STONES?**

**6** IN WHICH MAJOR GAME DID *CITY* WEAR SCARLET SHIRTS NUMBERED 12 THROUGH 22?

**7** WHICH SHIRT NUMBER LINKS *DAVID BRIGHTWELL, JEFF WHITLEY, MICHAEL TARNAT, NIGEL CLOUGH, DANNY MILLS, GARETH BARRY, FRANK LAMPARD* AND *FABIAN DELPH?*

# BOSS MEN

**SIR MATT BUSBY**, THE MANAGER UNDER WHOM **MANCHESTER UNITED** BECAME THE FIRST ENGLISH TEAM TO WIN THE CHAMPIONS LEAGUE, WON THE FA CUP WITH **CITY** DURING HIS PLAYING DAYS.

IDENTIFY THESE OTHER **CITY** PLAYERS WHO BECAME TROPHY-WINNING MANAGERS WHEN THEIR PLAYING DAYS WERE OVER:

**1** IN THE 1990S, HE WON THE FOOTBALL LEAGUE SECOND DIVISION WITH **OLDHAM ATHLETIC**, THE FA CUP WITH **EVERTON** AND THE FOOTBALL LEAGUE SECOND DIVISION PLAY-OFFS WITH **CITY**.

**2** HAVING WON HONOURS WITH **WYCOMBE WANDERERS**, HE WON TWO LEAGUE CUPS WITH **LEICESTER CITY** AND NUMEROUS HONOURS WITH **CELTIC**, INCLUDING THREE LEAGUE TITLES.

**3** WON TWO FIRST DIVISION TITLES WITH **SUNDERLAND** IN THE 1990S AND THE VFF CUP WITH **THAILAND**.

**4** STEERED **CITY** TO THE 1956 FA CUP WIN.

**5** HE WON EIGHT MAJOR HONOURS WITH **LEEDS UNITED**.

**6** MANAGED THE 1976 LEAGUE CUP-WINNING TEAM.

**7** HE WON FIVE LEAGUE TITLES, FOUR SCOTTISH CUPS, AND A SCOTTISH LEAGUE CUP DURING TWO SPELLS IN CHARGE OF **CELTIC**.

**8** WON THE 1996 FOOTBALL LEAGUE SECOND DIVISION WITH **SWINDON TOWN** AND TWO FOOTBALL LEAGUE TROPHIES DURING HIS TIME IN CHARGE OF **BLACKPOOL**.

**9** WON THE FOOTBALL LEAGUE CHAMPIONSHIP WITH BOTH **SUNDERLAND** AND **WOLVERHAMPTON WANDERERS**.

**10** GUIDED **NORTHAMPTON TOWN** TO VICTORY IN THE 2020 LEAGUE TWO PLAY-OFF FINAL.

# BACK OF THE NET!

BY THE SUMMER OF 2021, *CITY* HAD WON 15 OF THE 22 MAJOR FINALS THEY HAD CONTESTED DURING THE CLUB'S HISTORY. ONE OF THE MOST FAMOUS GOALS EVER SCORED FOR *CITY* IN A FINAL WAS *DENNIS TUEART'S* SPECTACULAR GAME-WINNING OVERHEAD KICK IN THE 1976 LEAGUE CUP FINAL 2-1 VICTORY OVER *NEWCASTLE UNITED*, AFTER *ALAN GOWLING* HAD CANCELLED OUT *CITY'S* OPENER FROM WINGER *PETER BARNES*.

NAME *CITY'S* GOALSCORERS IN THESE 14 OTHER VICTORIES IN MAJOR FINALS:

**1**  FA CUP 1903-04: 1 - 0 *BOLTON WANDERERS*

**2**  FA CUP 1933-34: 2 - 1 *PORTSMOUTH*

**3**  FA CUP 1955-56: 3 - 1 *BIRMINGHAM CITY*

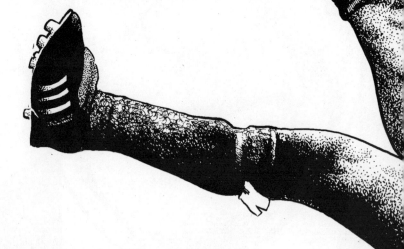

**4**  FA CUP 1968-69: 1 - 0 *LEICESTER CITY*

**5**  FOOTBALL LEAGUE CUP 1969-70: 2 - 1 *WEST BROMWICH ALBION*

**6**  UEFA CUP WINNERS' CUP 1969-70: 2 - 1 ***GÓRNIK ZABRZE***

**7**  FA CUP 2010-11: 1 - 0 ***STOKE CITY***

**8**  FOOTBALL LEAGUE CUP 2013-14: 3 - 1 ***SUNDERLAND***

**9**  FOOTBALL LEAGUE CUP 2015-16: 1 - 1 ***LIVERPOOL***
3 - 1 ON PENALTIES AFTER EXTRA-TIME

**10**  EFL CUP 2017-18: 3 - 0 ***ARSENAL***

**11**  EFL CUP 2018-19: 0 - 0 ***CHELSEA***
4 - 3 ON PENALTIES AFTER EXTRA-TIME

**12**  FA CUP 2018-19: 6 - 0 ***WATFORD***

**13**  EFL CUP 2019-20: 2 - 1 ***ASTON VILLA***

**14**  EFL CUP 2020-21: 1 - 0 ***TOTTENHAM HOTSPUR***

# THE NOTORIOUS KDB

ONE OF THE WORLD'S GREAT PLAYMAKERS, **KEVIN DE BRUYNE** WAS BORN IN DRONGEN, BELGIUM, ON JUNE 28, 1991. AS A KID HE WAS A **LIVERPOOL** FAN, WEARING A **LIVERPOOL** TRACKSUIT AND A **MICHAEL OWEN** REPLICA SHIRT AND EVEN SLEEPING IN **LIVERPOOL** BEDSHEETS!

**1**  WITH WHICH CLUB IN BELGIUM DID HE FIRST MAKE HIS MARK, WINNING BELGIAN LEAGUE, CUP AND SUPERCUP HONOURS?

**2**  HE SIGNED FOR **CHELSEA** IN JANUARY, 2012 AND JOINED THE CLUB THAT SUMMER. WHO WAS **CHELSEA** MANAGER WHEN **KEVIN** SIGNED AND WHO WAS MANAGER WHEN HE MADE HIS DEBUT IN JULY?

**3**  **CHELSEA** LOANED HIM OUT TO WHICH BUNDESLIGA TEAM?

**4**  HE RETURNED TO **CHELSEA** FOR SIX MONTHS BEFORE HIS £18 MILLION TRANSFER TO WHICH GERMAN CLUB IN EARLY 2014?

**5**  **DE BRUYNE** WAS NAMED 2015 PLAYER OF THE YEAR IN GERMANY. THE FOLLOWING YEAR, WHICH FORMER **CITY** PLAYER WON THE AWARD WHILE PLAYING FOR **BAYERN MUNICH?**

**6**  AFTER WINNING CUP AND SUPERCUP HONOURS IN GERMANY, HE JOINED **CITY** IN A CLUB RECORD £55 MILLION DEAL IN 2015. WHO WAS THE **CITY** MANAGER WHO SIGNED HIM?

**7**  IN 2020, HE EQUALLED WHOSE PREMIER LEAGUE RECORD OF 20 ASSISTS IN A SINGLE SEASON?

**8**  HE HAS WON THE PFA PLAYERS' PLAYER OF THE YEAR AWARD IN TWO CONSECUTIVE SEASONS. WHICH MANAGER OF **CITY** WON THE AWARD TWICE IN HIS PLAYING DAYS?

**9**  NAME THE THREE **BELGIUM** MANAGERS UNDER WHOM **KEVIN** HAS PLAYED HIS INTERNATIONAL FOOTBALL.

**10**  A COLLISION WITH WHICH **CHELSEA** PLAYER IN THE 2021 UEFA CHAMPIONS LEAGUE FINAL BROKE **KEVIN'S** NOSE AND EYE SOCKET?

# THE BOYS IN GREEN

**SHAY GIVEN** WAS BORN IN LIFFORD, COUNTY DONEGAL, ON APRIL 20, 1976. ALTHOUGH HE CONCEDED SEVEN GOALS ON HIS DEBUT, AT THE AGE OF 14, FOR LOCAL AMATEUR SIDE **LIFFORD CELTIC**, HE WAS SOON ON HIS WAY TO SCOTLAND TO SIGN FOR HIS BOYHOOD IDOLS, **CELTIC**. HE WENT ON TO WIN HONOURS WITH **SUNDERLAND, NEWCASTLE UNITED** AND **CITY**, AND RETIRED IN 2018 HAVING WON 134 INTERNATIONAL CAPS.

**1** WHICH **MANCHESTER CITY** DEFENDER HAS HAD TWO SPELLS AS MANAGER OF THE **REPUBLIC OF IRELAND**?

**2** IN THE ALL-TIME LIST OF **REPUBLIC OF IRELAND** GOALSCORERS, WHICH **CITY** STRIKER'S 21 GOALS PLACE HIM IN SECOND PLACE BEHIND **ROBBIE KEANE'S** 68-GOAL TALLY?

**3** WHICH **CITY** PLAYER'S **REPUBLIC OF IRELAND** CAREER ENDED IN CONTROVERSIAL CIRCUMSTANCES IN 2007 AMID REVELATIONS THAT HE HAD MISLED MANAGER **STEVE STAUNTON** ABOUT THE NEED FOR COMPASSIONATE LEAVE FROM THE TRAINING CAMP?

**4** WHICH FORMER **CITY** AND **REPUBLIC OF IRELAND** STRIKER VOICED AN UGLY SISTER IN SPANISH VERSIONS OF THE **"SHREK"** MOVIES?

**5** WHICH **REPUBLIC OF IRELAND** GOALKEEPER, WHO WAS **JOE CORRIGAN'S** UNDERSTUDY AT **CITY** BEFORE CLAIMING A REGULAR STARTING SLOT AT **CARDIFF CITY**, WAS LATER A PRISON OFFICER AT **HMP STYAL?**

**6** NAME THE STRIKER, A RECORD £5 MILLION SIGNING FROM **PRESTON NORTH END** IN 2002, WHO DURING HIS TIME WITH **CITY** EARNED THE ONLY **REPUBLIC OF IRELAND** CAP OF HIS CAREER.

**7** WHICH **REPUBLIC OF IRELAND** WINGER, WHO WON HONOURS WITH **NORTHAMPTON, CRYSTAL PALACE** AND **ARSENAL**, WAS THE ONLY SIGNING OF **STEVE COPPELL'S** 32-DAY **CITY** REIGN?

**8** FULL-BACK CAPPED 42 TIMES BY THE **REPUBLIC**, HE WON THE FA CUP WITH **WIMBLEDON**, PROMOTION WITH **FULHAM** AND SPENT A LITTLE OVER THREE SEASONS AT **CITY** BETWEEN 1992 AND 1995.

**9** DEFENDER CAPPED 80 TIMES WHILE PLAYING FOR **EVERTON, CITY, ASTON VILLA** AND **QUEENS PARK RANGERS**.

**10** MIDFIELDER CAPPED 20 TIMES BY THE **REPUBLIC OF IRELAND**, HE REACHED THE 1975 FA CUP FINAL WITH **FULHAM** BEFORE JOINING **CITY** THE FOLLOWING YEAR. HE LEFT IN 1978 FOR **PORTLAND TIMBERS** AND PLAYED AND COACHED EXTENSIVELY IN THE USA.

# BACK ROOM BOYS

WHEN **ROBERTO MANCINI** WAS INSTALLED AS **CITY** BOSS IN 2009, HE BROUGHT TWO FORMER TEAMMATES FROM HIS PLAYING DAYS AT **SAMPDORIA** -- **ENGLAND** INTERNATIONAL **DAVID PLATT** AND **ITALY** WINGER **ATTILIO LOMBARDO** -- ONTO THE COACHING STAFF. **LOMBARDO** CONTINUED TO WORK WITH **MANCINI** IN CLUB FOOTBALL AND IS HIS ASSISTANT MANAGER WITH THE ITALIAN NATIONAL TEAM.

IDENTIFY THESE OTHER **"BACK ROOM BOYS"**:

**1** FORMER **CITY, MANCHESTER UNITED** AND **ARSENAL** STAR, HE MANAGED **BLACKBURN ROVERS** IN HIS OWN RIGHT AND HAS ASSISTED AT **CITY, UNITED, LEEDS UNITED** AND **ENGLAND**.

**2** ASSISTANT MANAGER TO **PEP GUARDIOLA**, HE WAS APPOINTED **ARSENAL** MANAGER IN 2019.

**3** **ENGLAND** INTERNATIONAL WHO WAS ON THE COACHING STAFF UNDER **KEVIN KEEGAN** AND SUCCEEDED HIM AS MANAGER.

**4** **ENGLAND** DEFENDER WHO WAS ASSISTANT MANAGER TO **ENGLAND** BOSS **GRAHAM TAYLOR** BEFORE TAKING THE ASSISTANT **CITY** MANAGER JOB UNDER **STEVE COPPELL**. FOLLOWING THE SWIFT DEPARTURE OF **COPPELL**, HE WAS NAMED CARETAKER MANAGER UNTIL THE APPOINTMENT OF **FRANK CLARK**.

**5** LONG-TIME *CITY* CAPTAIN, HE WAS ON THE COACHING STAFF WHEN *MALCOLM ALLISON* LEFT IN 1973, BUT TURNED DOWN THE MANAGER JOB AND BECAME ASSISTANT TO EVENTUAL APPOINTEE *JOHNNY HART*. HE LATER BECAME *CITY'S* CHIEF SCOUT. HIS SON PLAYED FOR *ENGLAND* AND BOTH MANCHESTER CLUBS.

**6** *WREXHAM* AND *CHELSEA* GOALKEEPER, HE WORKED UNDER *MARK HUGHES* AT *WALES*, *BLACKBURN ROVERS*, *CITY*, *QUEENS PARK RANGERS*, *STOKE CITY* AND *SOUTHAMPTON*.

**7** *CITY* AND *SCOTLAND* FULL BACK, HE WAS ASSISTANT MANAGER TO *JOE ROYLE* AT *OLDHAM*, *CITY* AND *IPSWICH TOWN*.

**8** *SCOTLAND* INTERNATIONAL WHO MANAGED *STOCKPORT COUNTY*, HE WAS ASSISTANT TO *ALAN BALL* AND BRIEFLY CARETAKER MANAGER, AND THEN *CITY* RESERVE TEAM COACH.

**9** LONG-TIME *OLDHAM ATHLETIC* BOSS, HE WAS ASSISTANT MANAGER AND THEN SUCCESSOR TO *BILLY MCNEILL* AT *CITY*.

**10** WORLD CUP-WINNING PLAYER WHO BECAME BOSS OF *CITY'S* *ELITE DEVELOPMENT SQUAD* BEFORE MANAGING *NEW YORK CITY FC* AND *NICE*.

# THE PARATROOPER

**BERT TRAUTMANN**, THE FORMER PRISONER OF WAR WHO BECAME A LEGENDARY **CITY** GOALKEEPER, FAMED FOR PLAYING ON WITH A BROKEN NECK IN THE 1956 FA CUP FINAL, WAS PROBABLY THE ONLY FOOTBALLER TO RECEIVE THE IRON CROSS AND AN OBE FROM **THE QUEEN!** HE WAS AWARDED THE FORMER AFTER SERVING AS A CORPORAL WITH THE GERMAN ARMY'S 35TH INFANTRY DIVISION ON THE EASTERN FRONT IN THE SECOND WORLD WAR. AFTER RECEIVING THE LATTER, HONOURED FOR HIS WORK IN FURTHERING ANGLO-GERMAN RELATIONS, HE WAS INTRODUCED TO **QUEEN ELIZABETH** AT A 2004 RECEPTION AT THE BRITISH EMBASSY IN BERLIN. **"AH, HERR TRAUTMANN. I REMEMBER YOU"**, SHE REMARKED. **"HAVE YOU STILL GOT THAT PAIN IN YOUR NECK?"**

**1**  **BERT TRAUTMANN** WAS BORN IN THE GERMAN CITY OF:
A) BERLIN   B) BREMEN   C) BONN   D) BREMERHAVEN.

**2**  BROUGHT TO BRITAIN AS A P.O.W. FOLLOWING THE SECOND WORLD WAR, HE BEGAN HIS GOALKEEPING CAREER WITH WHICH NON-LEAGUE LANCASHIRE TEAM?

**3**  NAME THE MANAGER, A FORMER LEAGUE AND FA CUP WINNER WITH **EVERTON** AS A PLAYER, WHO SIGNED **TRAUTMANN** TO **MANCHESTER CITY** IN 1949.

**4**  IN 1956, **TRAUTMANN** BECAME THE SECOND **CITY** PLAYER TO BE NAMED FOOTBALLER OF THE YEAR. WHO WAS THE FIRST?

**5**  AFTER LEAVING CITY IN 1964, **TRAUTMANN** SIGNED FOR **WELLINGTON TOWN**. HOW WAS THAT CLUB RENAMED IN 1969?

**6**  WITH WHICH NORTHERN CLUB DID HE BEGIN HIS COACHING CAREER?

**7**  AS A COACH, **BERT** TOOK WHICH TEAM TO THE 1972 OLYMPICS?

**8**  NAME ONE OF THE FOUR OTHER INTERNATIONAL TEAMS HE MANAGED.

**9**  IN WHICH COUNTRY WAS **TRAUTMANN** LIVING AT THE TIME OF HIS DEATH IN 2013?

**10** GERMAN ACTOR
*DAVID KROSS*
PLAYED *BERT*
*TRAUTMANN*
IN A 2018 BIOPIC,
RELEASED
UNDER THE TITLE
*"TRAUTMANN"*
IN GERMANY,
WHAT WAS THE
FILM'S TITLE IN
BRITAIN?

# BONDED TO BOND

ALTHOUGH SIGNED TO *CITY* FOR £1 MILLION BY *MALCOLM ALLISON*, *KEVIN REEVES* SOON FOUND HIMSELF PLAYING FOR *JOHN BOND*, UNDER WHOM HE HAD PLAYED AT HIS FIRST TWO CLUBS, *BOURNEMOUTH* AND *NORWICH CITY*. HE SUBSEQUENTLY PLAYED FOR *BOND* AT *BURNLEY* AND WHEN A HIP INJURY ENDED HIS CAREER AT THE AGE OF 26, COACHED UNDER *BOND* AT *BURNLEY* AND *BIRMINGHAM CITY*.

NAME THESE PLAYERS WHO JOINED *CITY* DURING *JOHN BOND'S* TENURE:

**1** SCOTTISH MIDFIELD ENFORCER SIGNED FROM *BRISTOL CITY*, FOR WHOM HE HAD MADE 440 APPEARANCES, HE SUBSEQUENTLY PLAYED FOR *DONCASTER ROVERS* AND *BURNLEY* AND MANAGED *YEOVIL TOWN* AND *WEYMOUTH*.

**2** *NORTHERN IRELAND* MIDFIELDER, HE WON TWO EUROPEAN CUPS AND A LEAGUE TITLE WITH *NOTTINGHAM FOREST*, A CLUB HE SUBSEQUENTLY MANAGED AFTER MANAGEMENT SPELLS WITH CLUBS INCLUDING *WYCOMBE WANDERERS, LEICESTER CITY, CELTIC* AND *ASTON VILLA* AND THE *NORTHERN IRELAND* TEAM.

**3** NORWEGIAN DEFENDER WHO LATER MANAGED *NORWAY, DENMARK* AND A NUMBER OF SCANDINAVIAN TEAMS.

**4** MUCH-TRAVELLED STRIKER WHO WON PROMOTION WITH *NORWICH CITY*, AND PROMOTION, THE SECOND DIVISION GOLDEN BOOT AND THE FA CUP WITH *WEST HAM UNITED*.

**5** SIGNED FROM *TOTTENHAM HOTSPUR*, HE PLAYED JUST THREE GAMES FOR *CITY* BEFORE JOINING *CRYSTAL PALACE* TWO MONTHS LATER.

**6** STRIKER CAPPED ONCE BY *ENGLAND*, HE PLAYED MORE THAN 100 TIMES FOR FOUR CLUBS -- *YORK CITY, BOURNEMOUTH, NORWICH CITY* AND *SOUTHAMPTON* -- AND WAS FIRST DIVISION TOP SCORER THE SEASON BEFORE JOINING *CITY*.

**7** SIGNED FROM *SEATTLE SOUNDERS*, HE LATER MANAGED IN HIS OWN RIGHT AS WELL BEING AN ASSISTANT MANAGER UNDER *ALAN BALL, HARRY REDKNAPP* AND *GLENN ROEDER*.

**8** SIGNED FOR £1.2 MILLION FROM *NOTTINGHAM FOREST*.

**9** FULL-BACK WHO HAD PLAYED FOR *BOND* AT *NORWICH* AND WAS SIGNED FROM *SHEFFIELD UNITED* WEEKS BEFORE TURNING 35.

**10** *SCOTLAND* INTERNATIONAL WINGER WHO PLAYED MORE THAN 1,000 GAMES, CONTINUING INTO HIS MID-40S, HE SCORED FOR BOTH SIDES IN THE 1981 FA CUP FINAL!

# STERLING STUFF

SIGNED IN 2015, *RAHEEM STERLING* HELPED *CITY* WIN BACK-TO-BACK PREMIER LEAGUE TITLES IN THE 2017-18 AND 2018-19 SEASONS. HIS INDIVIDUAL HONOURS INCLUDE THE PFA YOUNG PLAYER OF THE YEAR AND FWA FOOTBALLER OF THE YEAR AWARDS.

**1** *RAHEEM STERLING* WAS BORN IN WHICH COUNTRY?
A) BARBADOS   B) BERMUDA   C) GRENADA   D) JAMAICA

**2** WHICH BASKETBALL SUPERSTAR INSPIRED *RAHEEM'S* MIDDLE NAME?

**3** HE JOINED WHICH LONDON CLUB AT THE AGE OF 10?

**4** WHO WAS THE MANAGER WHO SIGNED HIM TO *LIVERPOOL* IN 2010?

**5** IN HIS FOURTH APPEARANCE FOR *ENGLAND*, HE WAS RED CARDED ALONG WITH WHICH *ECUADOR* AND *MANCHESTER UNITED* STAR?

**6** *RAHEEM* WON THE GOLDEN BOY AWARD IN 2014 -- IN 2004, WHO WAS THE FIRST *ENGLAND* INTERNATIONAL TO WIN THE AWARD?

**7** HE JOINED *CITY* IN 2015, HIS TRANSFER FEE OF £44 MILLION PLUS £5 MILLION IN ADD-ONS MAKING HIM THE MOST EXPENSIVE ENGLISH PLAYER IN HISTORY. THE TRANSFER OF WHICH *ENGLAND* INTERNATIONAL TO *CITY* THE FOLLOWING YEAR EXCEEDED THAT?

**8** *RAHEEM* SCORED HIS FIRST HAT-TRICK FOR *CITY* IN A PREMIER LEAGUE GAME AGAINST WHICH TEAM IN OCTOBER 2015?

**9** HE SCORED HIS FIRST *ENGLAND* HAT-TRICK AGAINST WHICH NATION IN A 5-0 WIN AT WEMBLEY IN MARCH 2019?

**10** IN 2017, WHO WAS THE REFEREE WHO GAVE *STERLING* A SECOND YELLOW CARD FOR CELEBRATING AMONG THE TRAVELLING SUPPORTERS AFTER SCORING A STOPPAGE TIME WINNER AGAINST *BOURNEMOUTH?*

# 2006 WORLD CUP

**PAULO WANCHOPE'S** TWO GOALS AGAINST **GERMANY** IN THE OPENING GAME OF THE 2006 WORLD CUP MADE HM THE FIRST **COSTA RICA** PLAYER TO SCORE TWICE IN A WORLD CUP GAME. HE'D ARRIVED IN ENGLAND A DECADE EARLIER TO PLAY FOR **DERBY COUNTY**. TWO YEARS LATER, HE SIGNED FOR **WEST HAM UNITED**, AND A SEASON LATER, HE JOINED **MANCHESTER CITY**. THE CLUB WAS RELEGATED TO THE SECOND TIER IN HIS DEBUT SEASON, BUT BOUNCED BACK TO THE PREMIER LEAGUE THE FOLLOWING YEAR. HE WAS DOGGED BY INJURY DURING HIS TIME WITH **CITY**. HE SUBSEQUENTLY PLAYED FOR CLUBS IN SPAIN, QATAR, COSTA RICA, ARGENTINA, JAPAN AND THE UNITED STATES BEFORE RETIRING. MOVING INTO MANAGEMENT, HE TOOK OVER THE REINS OF THE **COSTA RICA** NATIONAL TEAM BUT RESIGNED IN 2015 AFTER A POST-GAME BRAWL.

**1** WHICH SUBSEQUENT **CITY** PLAYER, A **JUVENTUS** PLAYER AT THE TIME, SCORED TWICE FOR **FRANCE** IN THE 2006 WORLD CUP?

**2** **CARLOS TEVEZ** SCORED ONCE FOR **ARGENTINA** -- HE WOULD MOVE TO **WEST HAM UNITED** THE FOLLOWING MONTH, BUT WHICH BRAZILIAN CLUB WAS HE PLAYING FOR AT THAT TIME?

**3** **ENGLAND'S** 2006 WORLD CUP SQUAD CONTAINED A **MANCHESTER CITY** GOALKEEPER AND FOUR OTHER PLAYERS -- A GOALKEEPER, A FULL BACK AND TWO MIDFIELDERS -- WHO WOULD SUBSEQUENTLY PLAY FOR **CITY**. CAN YOU NAME THEM?

**4** THE **TOURÉ** BROTHERS WERE INCLUDED IN THE **IVORY COAST** SQUAD. KOLO WAS ON THE BOOKS AT ARSENAL -- BUT WHICH GREEK CLUB WAS **YAYA** SIGNED TO IN 2006?

**5** WHICH **PARAGUAY** STRIKER, A **BAYERN MUNICH** PLAYER IN 2006, WOULD LATER SIGN FOR **CITY?**

**6** **HATEM TRABELSI** WAS IN THE **TUNISIA** SQUAD. HE WOULD MOVE TO **CITY** LATER THAT SUMMER FROM WHICH DUTCH CLUB?

**7** **CITY'S CLAUDIO REYNA** WAS IN THE **UNITED STATES** SQUAD, AS WAS WHICH PLAYER, THEN WITH **PSV EINDHOVEN**, WHO WOULD

JOIN *CITY* WEEKS AFTER THE TOURNAMENT?

**8** WHICH COUNTRY DID *EMMANUEL ADEBAYOR* REPRESENT AT THE 2006 WORLD CUP?

**9** *BRAZIL'S ROBINHO* WAS PLAYING FOR WHICH CLUB IN 2006?

**10** WHICH SUBSEQUENT *CITY* BOSS MANAGED A TEAM AT THE 2006 WORLD CUP?

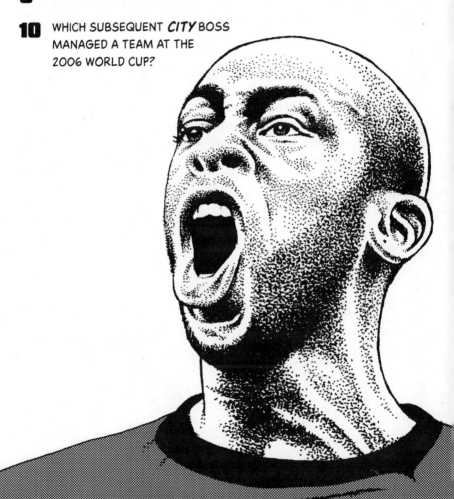

# THE GOAL MACHINE

BORN IN BUENOS AIRES, ARGENTINA, ON JUNE 2, 1988, **SERGIO AGÜERO** WAS GIVEN HIS **"KUN"** NICKNAME AT AN EARLY AGE BY HIS GRANDPARENTS. IT IS DERIVED FROM **"KUM-KUM"**, A CHARACTER ON HIS FAVOURITE ANIMATED CARTOON SHOW. AFTER TEN SEASONS WITH **CITY**, DURING WHICH TIME HE BECAME THE CLUB'S ALL-TIME RECORD GOALSCORER WITH 260 GOALS, HE JOINED **BARCELONA** IN THE SUMMER OF 2021,

**1** **SERGIO AGÜERO** BEGAN HIS CAREER WITH WHICH BUENOS AIRES-BASED CLUB?

**2** HE MADE HIS DEBUT IN THE ARGENTINE PRIMERA DIVISIÓN AT THE AGE OF 15 YEARS AND 35 DAYS, BREAKING THE RECORD PREVIOUSLY HELD BY WHICH PLAYER?

**3** HE JOINED WHICH EUROPEAN CLUB IN 2006?

**4** HE WON OLYMPIC GOLD AT THE 2008 BEIJING OLYMPICS. WHO DID **ARGENTINA** DEFEAT IN THE FINAL?

**5** HE SCORED TWICE IN HIS **CITY** DEBUT, IN A 4-0 PREMIER LEAGUE VICTORY OVER WHICH TEAM?

**6** **SERGIO** WORE WHICH NUMBER AT **CITY** BEFORE TAKING THE NUMBER 10 SHIRT?

**7** **SERGIO** IS CITY'S ALL-TIME LEADING SCORER, HAVING SURPASSED THE 177 GOAL TALLY OF WHICH PLAYER?

**8** HIS 184 PREMIER LEAGUE GOALS FOR **CITY** SURPASSED THE PREVIOUS RECORD OF MOST GOALS SCORED FOR A SINGLE PREMIER LEAGUE CLUB SET BY WHICH PLAYER?

**9** HE IS **ARGENTINA'S** THIRD-HIGHEST ALL-TIME TOP GOALSCORER, BEHIND WHICH TWO PLAYERS?

**10** NAME **SERGIO'S** SON -- THE ONLY CHILD OF HIS FOUR-YEAR MARRIAGE TO **DIEGO MARADONA'S** DAUGHTER, **GIANINNA** -- WHOSE NAME **SERGIO** HAS TATTOOED ON HIS ARM.

# WORLD CUP BOSSES

WITH **ENGLAND** HAVING FAILED TO QUALIFY FOR THE 1974 AND 1978 WORLD CUP TOURNAMENTS, THE 1982 WORLD CUP REPRESENTED THE FIRST -- AND PROBABLY LAST -- OPPORTUNITY FOR 31-YEAR-OLD **KEVIN KEEGAN** TO REPRESENT HIS COUNTRY ON THE WORLD STAGE. ALTHOUGH INJURED, **KEEGAN** WAS INCLUDED IN THE SQUAD BUT FAILED TO REGAIN FITNESS IN TIME TO PLAY IN THE GROUP GAMES. WITH 26 MINUTES LEFT IN A SECOND ROUND GAME AGAINST **SPAIN** THAT **ENGLAND** NEEDED TO WIN IN ORDER TO ADVANCE TO THE QUARTER-FINALS, **KEEGAN** WAS SENT ON AS A SUBSTITUTE ... AND MISSED AN EASY CHANCE THAT WOULD HAVE BROKEN THE DEADLOCK. **ENGLAND** WERE ELIMINATED AND THE SUPERSTAR'S DECADE-LONG **ENGLAND** CAREER WAS OVER.

IDENTIFY THESE OTHER FUTURE **CITY** MANAGERS AND CARETAKER MANAGERS WHO REPRESENTED THEIR COUNTRY AT THE WORLD CUP:

**1** WHICH **CITY** MANAGER WAS A WORLD CUP WINNER IN 1966?

**2** FOUR YEARS LATER, THAT SAME PLAYER WAS IN A WORLD CUP SQUAD WITH WHICH TWO **CITY** PLAYERS?

**3** WHICH SUBSEQUENT CARETAKER MANAGER OF **CITY** REPRESENTED HIS COUNTRY AT THE 1978 WORLD CUP?

**4** BESIDES **KEVIN KEEGAN,** WHICH THREE OTHER PLAYERS WHO WOULD LATER MANAGE **CITY** -- OR SERVE AS CARETAKER MANAGER -- REPRESENTED THEIR COUNTRY AT THE 1982 WORLD CUP?

**5** WHICH SUBSEQUENT **CITY** MANAGER WAS A MEMBER OF **ENGLAND'S** 1986 WORLD CUP SQUAD?

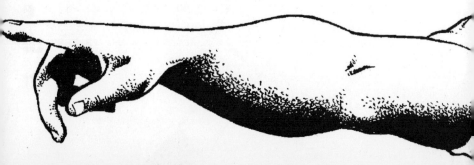

**6**   NAME THE SUBSEQUENT *CITY* MANAGER WHO WAS INCLUDED IN HIS COUNTRY'S 1990 WORLD CUP SQUAD BUT PLAYED NO MINUTES IN THE TOURNAMENT.

**7**   NAME THE FOUR SUBSEQUENT *CITY* PLAYERS, ONE OF WHOM WOULD ALSO MANAGE THE CLUB, WHO WERE PART OF *ENGLAND'S* SQUAD AT THE 1990 WORLD CUP.

**8**   UNDER *GRAHAM TURNER, ENGLAND* FAILED TO QUALIFY FOR THE 1994 WORLD CUP -- WHICH SUBSEQUENT *CITY* ASSISTANT MANAGER AND CARETAKER WAS HIS ASSISTANT?

**9**   WHICH *CITY* MANAGER PLAYED IN THE 1994 TOURNAMENT?

# "ALLEZ LES BLEUS!"

BORN IN MARSEILLES, ON JUNE 26, 1987, *SAMIR NASRI* WAS NINE YEARS OLD WHEN HE JOINED *MARSEILLE'S* ACADEMY, AND BY THE AGE OF 16 HE WAS PLAYING IN THE CLUB'S RESERVES. HE MADE HIS PROFESSIONAL DEBUT IN SEPTEMBER 2004 AT AGE 17 AGAINST *SOCHAUX*. IN HIS SIX SEASONS WITH *CITY* AFTER JOINING FROM *ARSENAL*, HE WON TWO PREMIER LEAGUE FINALS AND A LEAGUE CUP.

FROM WHICH CLUBS DID THESE FRENCH PLAYERS JOIN *CITY*?

1. BENJAMIN MENDY
2. ELIAQUIM MANGALA
3. BACARY SAGNA
4. OUSMANE DABO
5. ANTOINE SIBIERSKI
6. PATRICK VIEIRA
7. SYLVAIN DISTIN
8. GAËL CLICHY
9. LAURENT CHARVET
10. NICOLAS ANELKA

# CAMPEONES

**RÚBEN DIAS** ARRIVED AT **CITY** FROM **BENFICA** IN LATE SEPTEMBER, 2020, WITH THE SEASON ALREADY UNDERWAY. HE TOOK HIS PLACE IN THE TEAM ON THE HEELS OF THE 5-2 THUMPING **CITY** HAD RECEIVED DAYS EARLIER AT HOME TO **LEICESTER CITY** ... AND HIS IMPACT WAS DRAMATIC. **CITY** RALLIED TO END THE SEASON AS CHAMPIONS, WITH **DIAS** REWARDED FOR HIS LEADERSHIP AND DEFENSIVE EXCELLENCE WITH NUMEROUS AWARDS, INCLUDING THE FWA FOOTBALLER OF THE YEAR AWARD.

**DIAS** HAD PREVIOUSLY WON PORTUGAL'S PRIMEIRA LIGA WITH **BENFICA**. IDENTIFY THE TEAMS WITH WHICH THESE OTHER MEMBERS OF **CITY'S** 2020-21 PREMIER LEAGUE SQUAD HAD PREVIOUSLY WON LEAGUE TITLES:

**1**   **BERNARDO SILVA:**
   A) 2014 PRIMEIRA LIGA
   B) 2017 LIGUE 1

**2**   **EDERSON:** 2016 PRIMEIRA LIGA, 2017 PRIMEIRA LIGA

**3**   **JOÃO CANCELO:**
   A) 2014 PRIMEIRA LIGA
   B) 2019 SERIE A

**4**   **RIYAD MAHREZ:** 2016 PREMIER LEAGUE

**5**   **BENJAMIN MENDY:** 2017 LIGUE 1

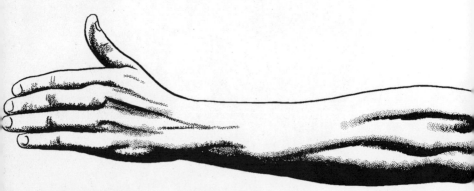

**6** ***FERNANDINHO:*** SIX UKRAINIAN PREMIER LEAGUES BETWEEN 2006 AND 2013

**7** ***KEVIN DE BRUYNE:*** 2011 BELGIAN PRO LEAGUE

**8** ***GABRIEL JESUS:*** CAMPEONATO BRASILEIRO SÉRIE A

**9** ***İLKAY GÜNDOĞAN:*** 2012 BUNDESLIGA

**10** ***KYLE WALKER:*** 2011 FOOTBALL LEAGUE CHAMPIONSHIP

# THE ONES THAT GOT AWAY

HAVING JOINED **WATFORD'S** ACADEMY AT THE AGE OF SEVEN, **JADON SANCHO** WAS SNAPPED UP BY **CITY** AT THE AGE OF 14, FOR AN INITIAL FEE OF £66,000 WITH THE POTENTIAL OF RISING TO £500,000 WITH ADD-ONS. HE IMPRESSED ENOUGH TO BE PUT ON THE FAST-TRACK TO THE SENIOR SQUAD ... BUT IMPATIENT FOR GAME TIME, HE ENGINEERED AN £8 MILLION MOVE TO **BORUSSIA DORTMUND** IN 2017.

**1** SIGNED TO *CITY'S* SCHOOL OF EXCELLENCE, WHO WAS POACHED BY *ALEX FERGUSON* ON HIS 14TH BIRTHDAY AND WENT ON TO WIN 13 LEAGUE TITLES AND TWO UEFA CHAMPIONS LEAGUES?

**2** FRENCH MIDFIELDER WHO WAS AT *CITY'S* ACADEMY AS A 13-YEAR OLD, HE WON FIVE LIGUE 1 TITLES WITH *PARIS SAINT-GERMAIN*, THE 2020 SERIE A WITH *JUVENTUS* AND IS A *FRANCE* REGULAR.

**3** HAVING MOVED TO *CITY* FROM *BARCELONA* AS A 17-YEAR-OLD, HE RETURNED TO THE CATALANS IN 2021 HAVING WON THE PREMIER LEAGUE AND LEAGUE CUP WITH THE SKY BLUES.

**4** *ENGLAND* FULL-BACK WHOSE ROUTE TO THE TOP TOOK HIM FROM *CITY'S* ACADEMY TO *BARNSLEY*, *TOTTENHAM HOTSPUR* AND ON TO A 2021 LA LIGA WINNER'S MEDAL WITH *ATLÉTICO MADRID*.

**5** *CITY* YOUNGSTER WHO PLAYED FOR *LEICESTER CITY* ON LOAN IN 2011 BEFORE BECOMING *BURNLEY'S* EVER-PRESENT CAPTAIN.

**6** YOUNG FORWARD WHO, HAVING MADE A SMATTERING OF APPEARANCES FOR *CITY*, SIGNED FOR *REAL MADRID* IN 2019 AND WON LA LIGA BEFORE JOINING *AC MILAN* ON LOAN IN 2020.

**7** *SWEDEN* STRIKER WHO WAS SENT OUT ON LOAN TO FIVE DIFFERENT CLUBS BETWEEN 2010 AND 2015, INCLUDING *CELTIC*, WITH WHOM HE WON A SCOTTISH LEAGUE AND LEAGUE CUP DOUBLE IN 2015.

**8** *REPUBLIC OF IRELAND* MIDFIELDER WHO MADE NO APPEARANCES FOR *CITY* BEFORE LAUNCHING HIS CAREER WITH *LEEDS UNITED*, WON HONOURS WITH *SHEFFIELD WEDNESDAY* AND *BOLTON WANDERERS* AND THEN EMBARKED ON AN EXTENSIVE MANAGEMENT CAREER.

**9** SPANIARD VOTED *CITY'S* YOUNG PLAYER OF THE YEAR IN 2012, HE SIGNED FOR *BARCELONA* IN 2013, AND HAS SUBSEQUENTLY PLAYED FOR *SEVILLA*, *VILLARREAL*, *ARSENAL* AND *CELTA VIGO*.

**10** *BELGIAN* INTERNATIONAL CENTRE-BACK, HE WON HONOURS WITH *CELTIC* AND *GALATASARAY* WHILE OUT ON LOAN FROM *CITY* BEFORE SIGNING FOR *OLYMPIQUE LYONNAIS* IN 2018.

# "SAFE HANDS" SEAMAN

ENGLAND'S SECOND MOST-CAPPED GOALKEEPER, ROTHERHAM-BORN *DAVID SEAMAN* WON A HOST OF AWARDS WITH *ARSENAL* BEFORE ENDING HIS PLAYING DAYS WITH A BRIEF SPELL AT *CITY* IN THE 2003-04 SEASON.

**1** HE BEGAN HIS CAREER WITH WHICH YORKSHIRE CLUB BUT WAS RELEASED IN 1982 BY MANAGER *EDDIE GRAY?*

**2** HE DROPPED DOWN TO THE FOURTH TIER TO PLAY FOR WHICH CLUB, WHOSE NICKNAME IS *"THE POSH"?*

**3** WHICH FORMER *MANCHESTER CITY* MANAGER SIGNED *SEAMAN* TO *BIRMINGHAM CITY* IN 1984?

**4** WHEN **BIRMINGHAM** WERE RELEGATED AFTER JUST ONE SEASON BACK IN THE TOP FLIGHT, WHICH MANAGER -- NICKNAMED **"THE BALD EAGLE"** -- SIGNED HIM TO **QUEENS PARK RANGERS?**

**5** HE EARNED HIS FIRST **ENGLAND** CAP IN NOVEMBER 1988 WHILE PLAYING FOR **QPR** -- WHO WAS THE **ENGLAND** MANAGER?

**6** WHEN **SEAMAN** JOINED **ARSENAL** IN 1990, HIS £1.3 MILLION TRANSFER FEE WAS A BRITISH RECORD FOR A GOALKEEPER. WHO WAS THE **ARSENAL** MANAGER WHO SIGNED HIM?

**7** HE WON THREE LEAGUE TITLES, FOUR FA CUPS AND THE LEAGUE CUP WITH **"THE GUNNERS"** -- AND THE 1994 EUROPEAN CUP WINNERS' CUP WHEN **ARSENAL** BEAT WHICH TEAM IN THE FINAL?

**8** WHO WAS THE MANAGER WHO SIGNED **SEAMAN** TO **CITY** IN 2003?

**9** HE BRIEFLY REPLACED **GARY LINEKER** AS CAPTAIN ON WHICH TV QUIZ SHOW BEFORE HE HIMSELF WAS REPLACED BY **IAN WRIGHT?**

**10** HOW MANY **ENGLAND** CAPS DID **DAVID SEAMAN** WIN?
A) 55  B) 75  C) 95

# CAPTAINS FANTASTIC

BESIDES THE FOUR PREMIER LEAGUE TITLES **VINCENT KOMPANY**
WON WITH **CITY**, HE ALSO WON SIX DOMESTIC CUPS -- FIVE OF THEM AS
CAPTAIN. NAME THE CAPTAINS WHO LED **CITY** IN THESE FINAL VICTORIES:

**1** 1904 FA CUP

**2** 1934 FA CUP

**3** 1956 FA CUP

**4** 1969 FA CUP

**5** 1970 UEFA CUP WINNERS' CUP

**6** 1970 LEAGUE CUP

**7** 1976 LEAGUE CUP

**8** 2011 FA CUP

**9** 2020 LEAGUE CUP

**10** 2021 LEAGUE CUP

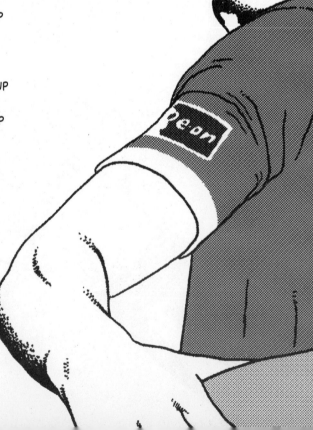

# THE LAWMAN

CAPPED 55 TIMES BY *SCOTLAND*, *DENIS LAW* HAD TWO SPELLS AT *CITY* -- THE FIRST DURING HIS METEORIC RISE TO BECOME A BALLON D'OR WINNER, AND THE SECOND IN THE TWILIGHT OF HIS CAREER AFTER YEARS OF GLORY WITH *MANCHESTER UNITED*, DURING WHICH TIME HE WON TWO LEAGUE TITLES, THE FA CUP, THE EUROPEAN CUP (ALTHOUGH INJURY RULED HIM OUT OF THE ACTUAL FINAL) AND THE BALLON D'OR. AFTER REJOINING *CITY*, HE SCORED THE FAMOUS BACKHEEL GOAL AGAINST HIS OLD CLUB IN THE LAST GAME OF THE 1973-74 SEASON IN WHICH THE REDS WERE RELEGATED.

**1** DESPITE BEING BRANDED BY THE CLUB AS *"WEAK, PUNY AND BESPECTACLED"*, *DENIS LAW* MADE HIS LEAGUE DEBUT FOR WHICH YORKSHIRE CLUB AT THE AGE OF 16 IN 1956?

**2** BETWEEN 1957 AND 1959, HE PLAYED UNDER WHICH SUBSEQUENT MANAGER OF *LIVERPOOL?*

**3** WHO WAS THE MANAGER WHO SIGNED HIM TO *CITY* IN 1960 FOR A RECORD FEE OF £55,000?

**4** HE JOINED WHICH ITALIAN CLUB IN 1961?

**5** HE JOINED *UNITED* IN 1962 FOR A RECORD FEE OF £115,000 -- WHO WAS THE FORMER *CITY* PLAYER WHO SIGNED HIM?

**6** WHO WAS THE *CITY* MANAGER WHO SIGNED *LAW* ON A FREE TRANSFER IN 1973? *LAW* RETIRED IN 1974.

**7** *LAW* HOLDS THE ALL-TIME *SCOTLAND* SCORING RECORD OF 30 GOALS JOINTLY WITH WHICH FORMER *CELTIC* AND *LIVERPOOL* PLAYER?

**8** HE WAS AN INAUGURAL INDUCTEE INTO THE ENGLISH FOOTBALL HALL OF FAME IN 2002 ALONG WITH WHICH OTHER FORMER *CITY* PLAYER?

**9** HE REPRESENTED *SCOTLAND* AT ONE WORLD CUP TOURNAMENT --
IN WHICH YEAR?

**10** *LAW* RECEIVED THE FREEDOM OF WHICH CITY OF HIS BIRTH IN 2017?

# IN SEARCH OF A TITLE

A GREAT SERVANT TO THE CLUB OVER 447 GAMES IN ELEVEN YEARS, *PAUL POWER* LED *CITY* OUT THREE TIMES AT WEMBLEY IN MAJOR FINALS AND ALWAYS LEFT EMPTY-HANDED. HE JOINED *EVERTON* IN 1986 AND WON THE FIRST MAJOR HONOUR OF HIS CAREER, HELPING *"THE TOFFEES"* TO THE LEAGUE TITLE IN HIS DEBUT SEASON.

IDENTIFY THESE OTHER PLAYERS WHO WON A LEAGUE TITLE AFTER LEAVING *CITY:*

**1** JOINED *LIVERPOOL* ON A FREE TRANSFER IN 2015 AND WON ANOTHER PREMIER LEAGUE TITLE TO ADD TO THE TWO HE WON WITH *CITY.*

**2** LEAGUE, FA CUP, LEAGUE CUP AND EUROPEAN CUP WINNERS' CUP WINNER WITH *CITY*, HE LEFT WITH A POINT TO PROVE IN 1974 -- AND MADE IT BY HELPING *DERBY COUNTY* WIN THE LEAGUE IN HIS DEBUT SEASON.

**3** A SECOND DIVISION AND FA CUP WINNER WITH *CITY*, HE SIGNED FOR UNITED IN 1906, WINNING TWO LEAGUE TITLES AND THE FA CUP WITH *MANCHESTER UNITED* BEFORE RETURNING TO *CITY* IN 1921.

**4** HE GAINED WINNER'S MEDALS IN THE FA CUP, LEAGUE CUP AND EUROPEAN CUP WINNERS' CUP WITH *CITY*, BEFORE WINNING THE LEAGUE, TWO FOOTBALL LEAGUE CUPS, TWO EUROPEAN CUPS AND MORE WITH *NOTTINGHAM FOREST.*

**5** AFTER LEAVING *CITY*, THIS *SCOTLAND* CAPTAIN WON A PREMIER LEAGUE TITLE WITH *BLACKBURN ROVERS* AND A SCOTTISH DOMESTIC TREBLE WITH *RANGERS.*

**6** AN EXPENSIVE MISFIT WITH *CITY,* A STRIKER WHO WON A TREBLE OF LEAGUE, LEAGUE CUP AND EUROPEAN CUP WITH *LIVERPOOL* IN 1984 BEFORE MAKING A CAREER AND LIFE IN SPAIN.

**7** *ENGLAND* STRIKER, A PROMISING YOUNGSTER AT *CITY* WHO LEFT FOR *CHELSEA* WHEN HIS CONTRACT EXPIRED IN 2009, HIS FEE DECIDED BY A TRIBUNAL. HE WON LEAGUE, FA CUP AND UEFA

CHAMPIONS LEAGUE HONOURS WITH THE LONDONERS AND A UEFA
CHAMPIONS LEAGUE WITH **LIVERPOOL**.

**8**   GOALKEEPER WHO LEFT **CITY** IN 2009 AND WENT ON TO WIN
PREMIER LEAGUE AND FA CUP MEDALS WITH **LEICESTER CITY**.

**9**   HE LEFT **CITY** IN 1930 AS THE CLUB'S ALL-TIME TOP GOALSCORER
AND NOT ONLY WON A LEAGUE TITLE WITH **EVERTON**, HE PLAYED IN
THE TEAM THAT BEAT HIS OLD CLUB IN THE 1933 FA CUP FINAL.

**10**   HAVING WON THE LEAGUE AND FA CUP DOUBLE WITH **ARSENAL**, HE
SPENT THREE FRUITLESS SEASONS WITH **CITY** BEFORE WINNING THE
DOUBLE WITH **CHELSEA** IN 2010.

# GOLDEN GLOVES HART

FOUR-TIME PREMIER LEAGUE GOLDEN GLOVE WINNER, CAPPED 75 TIMES BY *ENGLAND*, WHEN GOALKEEPER *JOE HART* LEFT *CITY* AFTER 12 SEASONS, CHAIRMAN *KHALDOON AL MUBARAK* SAID:
*"HE WILL RIGHTLY BE REGARDED AS A CITY LEGEND IN PERPETUITY".*

**1** *HART* BEGAN HIS CAREER WITH WHICH LOCAL SHROPSHIRE TEAM?

**2** HE JOINED *CITY* IN 2006 AND SPENT MUCH OF HIS DEBUT SEASON OUT ON LOAN AT TWO LOWER LEAGUE CLUBS -- NAME ONE.

**3** ON *HART'S* RETURN TO *CITY*, *SVEN-GÖRAN ERIKSSON* NAMED HIM AS NUMBER ONE AHEAD OF WHICH SWEDISH GOALKEEPER?

**4** UNDER MANAGER *MARK HUGHES*, *HART* FELL DOWN THE PECKING ORDER ON THE ARRIVAL OF WHICH GOALKEEPER IN EARLY 2009?

**5** *JOE* SPENT THE 2009-10 SEASON ON LOAN AT WHICH PREMIER LEAGUE CLUB?

**6** FOLLOWING THE APPOINTMENT OF *PEP GUARDIOLA* AS *CITY* MANAGER, *HART* WAS LOANED OUT TO WHICH ITALIAN CLUB?

**7** THE 2017-18 SEASON SAW HIM LOANED TO WHICH LONDON CLUB?

**8** HE LEFT *CITY* IN 2018 AND SPENT TWO FRUSTRATING SEASONS WITH WHICH LANCASHIRE CLUB?

**9** *HART* JOINED WHICH LONDON CLUB ON A FREE TRANSFER IN 2020?

**10** *HART* SHARES THE RECORD OF FOUR PREMIER LEAGUE GOLDEN GLOVES WITH WHICH *CHELSEA* AND *ARSENAL* GOALKEEPER?

BARCLA
GOLDEN GL

# A RED-HEADED GENIUS

LONDONDERRY LAD **PETER DOHERTY** WORKED AS A BRICKLAYER AND A BUS CONDUCTOR WHILE HELPING **GLENTORAN** WIN THE IRISH CUP IN 1933, EARNING HIMSELF A TRANSFER TO ENGLAND'S **BLACKPOOL** IN THE PROCESS. WHEN **CITY** BROKE THE BANK TO SIGN HIM IN 1936, THE BRILLIANT INSIDE-LEFT JUSTIFIED THE HEFTY £10,000 TRANSFER FEE BY INSPIRING **CITY** TO THE CLUB'S FIRST-EVER LEAGUE TITLE IN 1937. RESTRICTED TO FRIENDLY GAMES DURING THE SECOND WORLD WAR -- IN WHICH HE SERVED IN THE RAF -- HE SIGNED FOR **DERBY COUNTY** IN 1945 AND WON THE 1946 FA CUP. FOLLOWING A SPELL WITH **HUDDERSFIELD TOWN**, HE JOINED **DONCASTER ROVERS** AS PLAYER/ MANAGER, STAYING WITH THE CLUB FOR 11 YEARS, AND LATER MANAGED **BRISTOL CITY**. BETWEEN 1951 AND 1962, HE MANAGED **NORTHERN IRELAND**, TAKING THEM TO THE 1958 WORLD CUP FINALS.

**DOHERTY** HAD WON 16 CAPS AS A PLAYER. NAME THESE **CITY** PLAYERS WHO PLAYED FOR **NORTHERN IRELAND:**

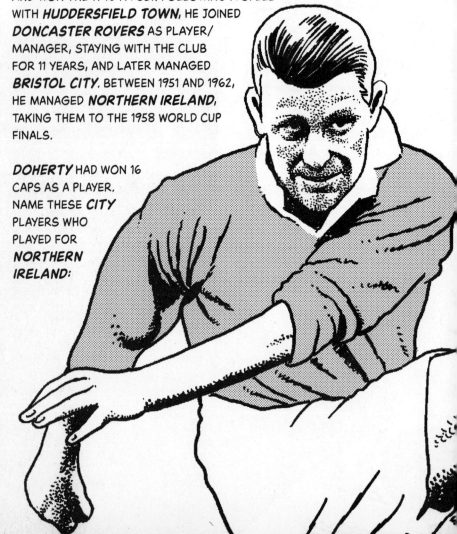

**1** CAPPED 88 TIMES, HE PLAYED FOR BOTH MANCHESTER CLUBS, **STOKE CITY** AND **BURY** AND MANAGED **NORTHERN IRELAND** BETWEEN 2000 AND 2003.

**2** HE WON TWO EUROPEAN CUPS AND A LEAGUE TITLE AS A PLAYER WITH **NOTTINGHAM FOREST**, WON MULTIPLE HONOURS AS MANAGER OF **LEICESTER CITY** AND CELTIC, AND WAS **REPUBLIC OF IRELAND** MANAGER FOR FIVE YEARS.

**3** INSIDE FORWARD WHO WON PROMOTION TO THE TOP FLIGHT WITH **SUNDERLAND** AND THEN CAPTAINED THE **CITY** TEAM THAT WON PROMOTION TO THE FIRST DIVISION IN 1967, BEFORE BEING SOLD TO **MIDDLESBROUGH**.

**4** AFTER WINNING HONOURS WITH **SWINDON TOWN**, HE WAS **FRANK CLARK'S** FIRST SIGNING FOR **CITY**. A PENALTY AND FREE-KICK EXPERT, IN SEVEN YEARS WITH **CITY** HE PLAYED IN THREE DIVISIONS, BEFORE JOINING **WEST HAM UNITED** IN 2003.

**5** NEPHEW OF **NORTHERN IRELAND** GOALKEEPER **HARRY GREGG**, HE WAS CAPPED 45 TIMES. HE SCORED AN OWN GOAL IN THE **LIVERPOOL** GAME THAT SAW **CITY** RELEGATED IN 1996, AND LATER PLAYED FOR **WEST HAM UNITED** AND **QUEENS PARK RANGERS**.

**6** CAPPED 40 TIMES, HE ENJOYED HIS GREATEST SUCCESSES AS A PLAYER AND SUBSEQUENT MANAGER WITH **CELTIC**, WINNING TEN LEAGUE TITLES OVERALL.

# CITY AND THE SAN SIRO

THERE ARE A NUMBER OF LINKS BETWEEN *CITY* AND THE TWO MILAN CLUBS, *AC MILAN* AND *INTERNAZIONALE*, WHO SHARE THE SAME STADIUM, THE STADIO GIUSEPPE MEAZZA, MORE COMMONLY KNOWN AS THE SAN SIRO.

**1** *ROBINHO* WON A SERIE A TITLE AND THE SUPERCOPPA ITALIANA WITH THE *"ROSSONERI"* FOLLOWING HIS 2010 TRANSFER FROM *CITY* TO *AC MILAN*. HE HAD LOAN SPELLS WITH WHICH CLUB WHILE ON THE BOOKS AT BOTH *CITY* AND *AC MILAN?*

**2** WHICH PLAYER WAS TRANSFERRED FROM *INTERNAZIONALE* TO *CITY* IN 2007, THEN TO *AC MILAN* THREE YEARS LATER?

**3** WHICH BRAZILIAN DEFENDER WON THE UEFA CHAMPIONS LEAGUE AND FOUR SERIE A TITLES WITH *INTERNAZIONALE*, THEN PLAYED ONE SEASON WITH *CITY* BEFORE JOINING *ROMA* IN 2013?

**4** *CITY* HAVE ONLY DRAWN MILANESE OPPOSITION IN EUROPE ON ONE OCCASION. IN 1978, THEY DREW 2-2 AGAINST *AC MILAN* IN THE SAN SIRO AND THEN BEAT THEM 3-0 AT MAINE ROAD TO ADVANCE TO THE QUARTER-FINAL OF THE UEFA CUP. WHICH SUBSEQUENT ASSISTANT MANAGER OF *CITY* SCORED A GOAL IN BOTH LEGS OF THE TIE?

**5** WHICH WORLD CUP-WINNING MIDFIELDER, WINNER OF MULTIPLE LEAGUE TITLES WITH *ARSENAL* AND *INTERNAZIONALE*, JOINED *CITY* FROM THE ITALIAN CLUB IN EARLY 2010?

**6** WHICH MIDFIELD ENFORCER LEFT *CITY* FOR *AC MILAN* IN 2012?

**7** WHICH *CITY* MANAGER HAS HAD TWO SPELLS IN CHARGE OF *INTERNAZIONALE*, WINNING THREE SERIE A TITLES AND MORE?

**8** WHO WAS THE *ENGLAND* INTERNATIONAL WHO PLAYED FOR BOTH MANCHESTER TEAMS, MANAGED *AC MILAN* FOR TWO YEARS IN THE 1920S, AND LATER TOOK CHARGE OF *PADOVA* AND *ROMA?*

**9** WHICH LEGENDARY LIBERIAN PLAYED FOR *MONACO*, *PARIS SAINT-GERMAN*, *AC MILAN*, *CHELSEA*, *CITY* AND *MARSEILLE?*

**10** NAME THE **MONTENEGRO** STRIKER WHO LEFT **CITY** FOR **INTERNAZIONALE** AFTER BEING OMITTED FROM **CITY'S** CHAMPIONS LEAGUE SQUAD?

# CHELSEA CONNECTIONS

THE CLUB'S ALL-TIME TOP GOALSCORER, WINNER OF THREE PREMIER LEAGUE TITLES, THE UEFA CHAMPIONS LEAGUE, THE UEFA EUROPA LEAGUE, FOUR FA CUPS, AND TWO FOOTBALL LEAGUE CUPS, **FRANK LAMPARD** LEFT **CHELSEA** AS A LEGEND, OSTENSIBLY TO JOIN **NEW YORK CITY FC**. HOWEVER, HE ENDED UP PLAYING A SEASON WITH **CITY** FIRST -- AND HE SCORED HIS FIRST GOAL FOR THE SKY BLUES, HAVING ONLY BEEN ON THE FIELD FOR SEVEN MINUTES, AGAINST **CHELSEA**!

**1** NAME THE ENGLAND FULL-BACK WHO JOINED **CITY** FROM **CHELSEA** IN 2009 AND FAMOUSLY REFUSED TO SHAKE HANDS WITH **CHELSEA'S JOHN TERRY** BEFORE A GAME THE FOLLOWING YEAR.

**2** WHICH **ENGLAND** INTERNATIONAL SPENT TWO SPELLS AT **CITY** BETWEEN FOUR SEASONS WITH **CHELSEA**, DURING WHICH TIME HE WON THE 2006 PREMIER LEAGUE AND THE 2007 FA CUP?

**3** **WEST BROMWICH ALBION** STRIKER WHO SCORED TWICE FOR **ENGLAND** AT THE 1958 WORLD CUP, HE FOLLOWED AN UNHAPPY FEW WEEKS AT **CHELSEA** UNDER **TOMMY DOCHERTY** BY SIGNING FOR **CITY**, FOR WHOM HE SCORED 56 GOALS IN 76 GAMES.

**4** CAPPED 96 TIMES BY **ISRAEL**, NAME THE CENTRE-BACK WHO JOINED **CITY** FROM **CHELSEA** IN 2007.

**5** NICKNAMED **"ROCKY"**, WHICH **ENGLAND** INTERNATIONAL WON TWO LEAGUE TITLES WITH **ARSENAL** AND PLAYED FOR **LEEDS UNITED**, **CITY, CHELSEA, NORWICH CITY** AND **HULL CITY**?

**6** **IPSWICH TOWN** PLAYER OF THE YEAR, WHICH SOUTH AFRICAN-BORN MIDFIELDER PLAYED TWICE FOR **ENGLAND** UNDER **DON REVIE** AND LEFT **CITY** FOR **CHELSEA** IN 1980?

**7** **CITY'S** GOALKEEPING HERO IN THE 2016 FOOTBALL LEAGUE CUP, WHICH **ARGENTINA** INTERNATIONAL JOINED **CHELSEA** ON A FREE, GOING ON TO WIN FA CUP, UEFA CHAMPIONS LEAGUE AND UEFA EUROPA LEAGUE MEDALS WITH THE LONDONERS?

**8** NAME THE STRIKER WHO PLAYED FOR SEVEN LONDON CLUBS AND SPENT TWO SEASONS AT *CITY* BETWEEN 1989 AND 1991.

**9** WHICH *WALES* INTERNATIONAL SET THE ALL-TIME GOALSCORING RECORD FOR *FULHAM* IN TWO SPELLS AT THE CLUB, IN BETWEEN WHICH HE PLAYED FOR *CHELSEA* AND *CITY* IN THE MID-1980S?

**10** WHICH DEFENDER, WHOSE REAL FIRST NAME IS *EUCLID*, SPENT EIGHT YEARS AT *CITY* BEFORE MOVING TO *CHELSEA* IN 1987 FOLLOWING RELEGATION AND LATER PLAYED FOR *QUEENS PARK RANGERS*, *TOTTENHAM HOTSPUR* AND *CAMBRIDGE UNITED*?

# KING OF THE KIPPAX

NICKNAMED **"THE KING OF THE KIPPAX"**, **COLIN BELL** IS UNIVERSALLY ACKNOWLEDGED AS ONE OF THE GREATEST PLAYERS EVER TO PULL ON A SKY BLUE SHIRT. THE WEST STAND OF THE CITY OF MANCHESTER STADIUM IS NAMED IN HIS HONOUR. **BELL** DIED IN 2021 AT THE AGE OF 74.

**1**   *COLIN BELL* WAS SIGNED TO *CITY* FROM WHICH CLUB IN 1966?

**2**   HIS NICKNAME WAS INSPIRED BY WHICH DERBY-WINNING RACEHORSE?

**3**   NAME THE FIVE MAJOR TROPHIES THAT *BELL* WON WITH *CITY*.

**4**   *BELL* WON 48 CAPS FOR *ENGLAND* BETWEEN 1968 AND 1975 -- UNDER WHICH THREE MANAGERS DID HE PLAY?

**5**   HE MADE THREE APPEARANCES AT THE 1970 WORLD CUP IN MEXICO, AFTER BEING OMITTED FROM THE SIDE THAT CONTESTED *ENGLAND'S* OPENING GAME AGAINST WHICH COUNTRY?

**6**   HIS CAREER WAS EFFECTIVELY CURTAILED FOLLOWING AN INJURY SUSTAINED IN A 1975 LEAGUE CUP GAME AGAINST WHICH CLUB?

**7**   NAME THE FIVE MANAGERS UNDER WHOM *BELL* PLAYED AT *CITY* BEFORE LEAVING THE CLUB IN 1979.

**8**   *BELL* BRIEFLY PLAYED WITH *GEORGE BEST* IN WHICH NASL SIDE IN THE UNITED STATES?

**9**   WHAT WAS THE TITLE OF HIS 2005 AUTOBIOGRAPHY?

**10**   HIS CHARITY WORK EARNED *BELL* AN APPOINTMENT TO WHICH RANK IN THE BRITISH ORDER OF CHIVALRY?

# "OOR WULLIE"

PLAYING FOR **SCOTLAND** AGAINST **WALES** IN 1978, **WILLIE DONACHIE** SCORED ONE OF FOOTBALL'S MOST INFAMOUS OWN GOALS! ATTEMPTING TO RUN DOWN THE CLOCK TO SECURE A 1-0 WIN, WITH NO OTHER PLAYER NEAR HIM, HIS BLIND BACKPASS FROM THE EDGE OF THE AREA LEFT HIS GOALKEEPER STRANDED AND FOUND THE BACK OF THE EMPTY NET! AFTER MAKING HIS DEBUT FOR **CITY** IN 1970, **WILLIE** MADE 431 APPEARANCES IN HIS TWO SPELLS AT THE CLUB, SCORING TWICE.

**1** **WILLIE** WON THE 1972 CHARITY SHIELD WHEN **CITY** BEAT **ASTON VILLA** 1-0. WHAT WAS UNUSUAL ABOUT THE GAME THAT YEAR?

**2** **WILLIE** REPLACED WHICH LONG-SERVING **CITY** LEFT-BACK?

**3** HE LEFT **CITY** IN 1980 FOR THE FIRST OF TWO SPELLS IN THE STATES WITH WHICH NASL TEAM?

**4** IN 1981-82, HE PLAYED WITH WHICH TEAM, WHERE **KEN BROWN** HAD RECENTLY SUCCEEDED **JOHN BOND** AS MANAGER?

**5** **WILLIE** PLAYED UNDER **JOHN BOND** AT WHICH LANCASHIRE CLUB?

**6** IN 1984, **WILLIE** BECAME PLAYER/ASSISTANT MANAGER UNDER **JOE ROYLE** AT WHICH CLUB, WINNING PROMOTION TO THE PREMIER LEAGUE AND REACHING THE 1990 LEAGUE CUP FINAL?

**7** **WILLIE** JOINED **ROYLE** ONCE MORE AS ASSISTANT MANAGER AT **EVERTON**, WHO DEFEATED WHICH TEAM TO WIN THE 1995 FA CUP?

**8** AFTER ASSISTING ROYLE AT CITY THEY LINKED UP AGAIN AT WHICH EAST ANGLIA CLUB?

**9** **WILLIE** SUCCEEDED **NIGEL SPACKMAN** AS MANAGER OF WHICH LONDON CLUB IN 2006?

**10** HAVING MANAGED AND COACHED A NUMBER OF TEAMS, INCLUDING **ANTIGUA AND BARBUDA**, HE WAS APPOINTED MANAGER OF WHICH CARIBBEAN ISLAND TEAM IN 2018 -- WHICH WAS HOME TO **GEORGE MARTIN'S AIR** RECORDING STUDIOS FOR MANY YEARS?

# HARTFORD'S HEART

IN 1971, YOUNG MIDFIELDER **ASA HARTFORD**, ONE OF THE HOTTEST PROPERTIES IN ENGLISH FOOTBALL, WAS ON THE VERGE OF JOINING **DON REVIE'S LEEDS UNITED** -- UNTIL THE ROUTINE MEDICAL REVEALED THAT HE HAD A TINY HOLE IN THE HEART. THE TRANSFER WAS ABRUPTLY CALLED OFF. AFTER RECEIVING EXPERT MEDICAL ADVICE, **HARTFORD** CONTINUED TO PLAY, EVENTUALLY WINNING 50 CAPS FOR **SCOTLAND**.

**1** WHICH CLUB WAS **HARTFORD** PLAYING FOR WHEN THE **LEEDS UNITED** TRANSFER FELL THROUGH?

**2** HE JOINED **CITY** IN 1974 AND WAS A HUGE FAVOURITE WITH THE FANS, UNTIL WHICH RETURNING MANAGER PUSHED HIM OUT IN 1979?

**3** HE SIGNED FOR WHICH CLUB AS THE INTENDED REPLACEMENT FOR **ARCHIE GEMMILL** BUT STAYED JUST A FEW WEEKS BEFORE JOINING **EVERTON?**

**4** **JOHN BOND** BROUGHT HIM BACK TO **CITY** IN 1981 BUT THE CLUB WAS RELEGATED IN 1983 UNDER WHICH MANAGER?

**5** HAVING PLAYED IN THE STATES WITH **FORT LAUDERDALE SUN**, HE RETURNED TO ENGLAND TO JOIN **NORWICH CITY**, WITH WHOM HE WON THE 1985 LEAGUE CUP AGAINST WHICH OPPONENTS?

**6** THAT SAME YEAR, HE SIGNED FOR **BOLTON WANDERERS**, WHERE HE PLAYED UNDER WHICH FORMER **ENGLAND** INTERNATIONAL, WHO WOULD SERVE AS **CITY'S** CARETAKER MANAGER A DECADE LATER?

**7** IN 1987, **ASA** SUCCEEDED **COLIN MURPHY** AS MANAGER OF WHICH FOURTH TIER CLUB?

**8** HE WORKED UNDER **JOE JORDAN** AND THEN **LOU MACARI** AT WHICH CLUB, WHERE HE ALSO BRIEFLY ASSUMED THE CARETAKER MANAGER ROLE IN 1994?

**9** HE RETURNED TO **CITY** IN THE MID-1990S AS ASSISTANT TO WHICH MANAGER, AFTER WHOSE DISMISSAL HE ACTED AS CARETAKER AND THEN STAYED ON AS A COACH UNTIL 2005?

**10** AT WHICH CLUB DID *ASA HARTFORD* ACT AS ASSISTANT MANAGER TO FORMER CITY DEFENDER *IAN BRIGHTWELL,* WHO WAS APPOINTED MANAGER AFTER THE SACKING OF FORMER *CITY* BOSS *BRIAN HORTON?*

# THE BOYS OF 2012

IN 2011-12, *CITY* WON THE TOP TIER TITLE FOR THE THIRD TIME IN THE CLUB'S 110-SEASON HISTORY AND THE FIRST TIME IN 44 YEARS. WITHIN WEEKS, SOME PLAYERS, INCLUDING *AC MILAN*-BOUND *NIGEL DE JONG*, HAD LEFT THE CLUB. BUT IT WASN'T UNTIL 2021 AND THE TRANSFER OF *SERGIO AGÜERO* TO *BARCELONA*, THAT THE LAST OF THE TITLE-WINNING SQUAD HAD LEFT *CITY*. FOR WHICH TEAM DID THE FOLLOWING MEMBERS OF THAT TITLE-WINNING SQUAD LEAVE:

1   MICAH RICHARDS

2   JOLEON LESCOTT

3   ALEKSANDAR KOLAROV

4   STEFAN SAVIĆ

5   GAËL CLICHY

6   ADAM JOHNSON

7   GARETH BARRY

8   KOLO TOURÉ

9   MARIO BALOTELLI

10  CARLOS TEVEZ

# 2014 WORLD CUP

IN *ITALY'S* OPENING GAME OF THE 2014 WORLD CUP, FORMER *CITY* STRIKER *MARIO BALOTELLI* SCORED THE WINNING GOAL AGAINST *ENGLAND* IN A 2-1 VICTORY. *ITALY* LOST THEIR NEXT TWO GROUP MATCHES AND WERE ELIMINATED FROM THE TOURNAMENT.

**1** WHICH SUBSEQUENT *CITY* STRIKER, THEN WITH *SWANSEA CITY*, SCORED TWICE FOR *IVORY COAST* AT THE TOURNAMENT?

**2** THE *BRAZIL* SQUAD CONTAINED ONE *CITY* PLAYER -- A DEFENSIVE MIDFIELDER -- ONE FORMER *CITY* FULL-BACK THEN PLAYING WITH *ROMA*, AND A STRIKER WHO HAD PLAYED FOR *CSKA MOSCOW*, *CITY*, *EVERTON* AND *GALATASARAY*. NAME ALL THREE.

**3** WHO WAS THE ONE FORMER *CITY* PLAYER IN *GERMANY'S* SQUAD?

**4** *SWITZERLAND'S* SQUAD CONTAINED WHICH EX-*CITY* PLAYER?

**5** *BELGIUM'S* SQUAD CONTAINED WHICH THREE PLAYERS WITH *CITY* CONNECTIONS -- A CURRENT CENTRE-BACK, ANOTHER WHO HAD PLAYED FOR THE CLUB IN 2004, AND A MIDFIELDER WHO WOULD JOIN THE SKY BLUES THE FOLLOWING YEAR?

**6** THE *ARGENTINA* SQUAD CONTAINED WHICH THREE *CITY* PLAYERS?

**7** FORMER *CITY* STRIKER *FELIPE CAICEDO* WAS A MEMBER OF WHICH NATION'S SQUAD?

**8** WHICH FORMER *CITY* STRIKER REPRESENTED *GREECE?*

**9** *ENGLAND'S* SQUAD FEATURED A *CITY* GOALKEEPER AND A MIDFIELDER, A FORMER *CITY* STRIKER AND A FUTURE *CITY* FORWARD WHO WERE BOTH *LIVERPOOL* PLAYERS AT THAT TIME, AND A MIDFIELDER WHO WOULD LEAVE *CHELSEA* FOR *CITY* THAT SUMMER. NAME ALL FIVE.

**10** WHO WAS THE ONLY FORMER *CITY* PLAYER IN THE *UNITED STATES* SQUAD?

# FRANNY LEE

*FRANCIS LEE* WON THE LEAGUE IN HIS DEBUT SEASON WITH *CITY*, THE FA CUP IN HIS SOPHOMORE SEASON AND THE LEAGUE CUP AND UEFA CUP WINNERS' CUP IN HIS THIRD.

**1** *FRANCIS LEE* JOINED *MANCHESTER CITY*, FOR A CLUB RECORD FEE OF £60,000, FROM WHICH CLUB IN 1967?

**2** *LEE'S* FIRST-HALF PENALTY HELPED SECURE A 2-1 WIN OVER *GÓRNIK ZABRZE* IN THE 1970 EUROPEAN CUP WINNERS' CUP FINAL. WHO SCORED *CITY'S* OTHER GOAL?

**3** WITH 10 GOALS, *LEE* SHARED THE RECORD FOR MOST GOALS SCORED IN A MANCHESTER DERBY WITH *CITY* GREAT *JOE HAYES*, UNTIL WHICH *MANCHESTER UNITED* PLAYER BETTERED THEIR TALLY IN 2013?

**4** OFF THE FIELD, *LEE* BECAME A MILLIONAIRE THANKS TO HIS TOILET ROLL MANUFACTURING BUSINESS. THE FIRM FAMOUSLY EMPLOYED WHICH SUBSEQUENT STAR COMEDIAN?

**5** *LEE* REPRESENTED *ENGLAND* IN THE 1970 WORLD CUP IN MEXICO, WHERE HE BECAME THE FIRST *ENGLAND* PLAYER TO RECEIVE A YELLOW CARD IN A WORLD CUP GAME. WHO WERE THE OPPONENTS?

**6** *LEE* JOINED *DERBY COUNTY* IN 1974 AND SUBSEQUENTLY WON HIS SECOND LEAGUE TITLE. WHO WAS THE MANAGER WHO SIGNED HIM TO THE CLUB AND DELIVERED THAT TITLE?

**7** *LEE'S* RED CARD IN A 1975 GAME AGAINST *LEEDS UNITED* WAS DESCRIBED BY THE OBSERVER AS *"SPORT'S MOST SPECTACULAR DISMISSAL"*. WHO WAS THE OTHER PLAYER RED-CARDED IN THAT INFAMOUS BRAWLING INCIDENT?

**8** WHO DID *LEE* REPLACE AS *MANCHESTER CITY* CHAIRMAN FOLLOWING A SUCCESSFUL TAKEOVER IN 1994?

**9** **BRIAN HORTON** WAS **MANCHESTER CITY** MANAGER WHEN **LEE** BECAME CHAIRMAN, AND **JOE ROYLE** WAS IN THE JOB WHEN **LEE** STEPPED DOWN IN 1998. NAME THE FIVE OTHERS, INCLUDING CARETAKERS, WHO FILLED THE ROLE IN THE INTERVENING YEARS.

**10** **LEE** WAS AWARDED A CBE IN THE 2016 NEW YEAR HONOURS LIST, AS WAS WHICH **MANCHESTER CITY** TEAMMATE?

# PROUD PEACOCKS

STRETFORD-BORN *JOHN SHERIDAN* LEFT *CITY* FOR *LEEDS UNITED* IN 1982 HAVING NEVER MADE HIS SENIOR DEBUT. HE SPENT SEVEN YEARS IN THE FIRST TEAM AT ELLAND ROAD, WON PROMOTION AND SCORED THE WINNING GOAL IN THE LEAGUE CUP FINAL DURING SEVEN YEARS WITH *SHEFFIELD WEDNESDAY*, AND WAS CAPPED 35 TIMES BY THE *REPUBLIC OF IRELAND* BEFORE BEGINNING A LENGTHY CAREER IN MANAGEMENT.

IDENTIFY THESE OTHERS WHO PLAYED FOR *CITY* AND *LEEDS UNITED*.

**1** WHICH FORMER *LEEDS UNITED* AND *ASTON VILLA* MIDFIELDER JOINED *CITY* IN EARLY 2015?

**2** PACY WINGER WHO JOINED *CITY* FROM *LEEDS UNITED* IN LATE 2000, EXPERIENCED RELEGATION AND PROMOTION, AND LATER BECAME A *NORWICH CITY* HALL OF FAMER.

**3** *ENGLAND'S* RIGHT-BACK AT THE 2002 WORLD CUP, HE LEFT *LEEDS UNITED* FOR *CITY* IN 2004, HAVING WON A LEAGUE CUP ON LOAN AT *MIDDLESBROUGH*.

**4** FA CUP WINNER WITH *CITY* IN 1956, AN FWA FOOTBALLER OF THE YEAR WHO ENDED HIS PLAYING CAREER AT *LEEDS UNITED* BEFORE BECOMING ONE OF THE CLUB'S MOST SUCCESSFUL MANAGERS.

**5** WINGER WHO, AFTER EIGHT SUCCESSFUL YEARS AT *CITY* -- DURING WHICH TIME HE WON HIS SOLITARY *ENGLAND* CAP -- MOVED ON TO *LEEDS UNITED* IN 1993 THEN *SHEFFIELD UNITED*.

**6** DEFENDER WHO RACKED UP MORE THAN 600 GAMES IN A 20-YEAR CAREER THAT SAW HIM PLAY FOR A NUMBER OF CLUBS, INCLUDING *HULL CITY* AND *LEEDS UNITED*, PLAY UNDER *JOE ROYLE* AT *OLDHAM ATHLETIC* AND *CITY*, AND LATER SPEND A PERIOD AS CHAIRMAN OF THE PROFESSIONAL FOOTBALLERS' ASSOCIATION.

**7** *SCOTLAND* STRIKER WHO WON MULTIPLE HONOURS WITH *RANGERS*, INCLUDING THE 1972 EUROPEAN CUP WINNERS' CUP, HE JOINED *CITY* FROM *LEEDS UNITED* IN 1983.

**8** CAPPED 34 TIMES BY *NORWAY*, HE LEFT *LEEDS UNITED* FOR *CITY* IN 2000 BUT HIS CAREER WAS CURTAILED BY INJURY.

**9** SCOTTISH FULL-BACK WHO MADE 161 CONSECUTIVE LEAGUE APPEARANCES FOR *COVENTRY CITY*, PLAYED IN THE 1981 CUP FINAL FOR *MANCHESTER CITY*, WON TWO PROMOTIONS WITH *OXFORD UNITED* AND SIGNED FOR *LEEDS UNITED* IN 1987.

**10** CAPPED 22 TIMES BY *ENGLAND*, HE SCORED IN THE 1976 LEAGUE CUP FINAL WIN DURING ONE OF TWO SPELLS WITH *CITY*, HAD TWO SPELLS WITH *MANCHESTER UNITED* AND TWO SPELLS WITH *LEEDS UNITED* IN A CAREER THAT ALSO SAW HIM PLAY IN SPAIN, PORTUGAL, AUSTRALIA, MALTA, THE UNITED STATES AND IRELAND.

# CITY'S DRAGONS

HAVING REPRESENTED **WALES** AT YOUTH LEVELS, CARDIFF NATIVE **CRAIG BELLAMY** EARNED THE FIRST OF HIS 78 CAPS AT THE AGE OF 18. HE ALSO CAPTAINED THE NATIONAL TEAM FROM 2007 TO 2011.

IDENTIFY THESE **CITY** PLAYERS CAPPED BY **WALES**.

**1** A RHONDDA VALLEY MINER BEFORE TURNING PRO WITH **SWANSEA TOWN**, CAPPED 33 TIMES, HE CAPTAINED **CITY'S** FA CUP FINAL SIDES IN 1955 AND 1956.

**2** DEFENDER CAPPED 36 TIMES BETWEEN 1992 AND 2001, HE PLAYED FOR **PORTSMOUTH, CITY, FULHAM** AND **CRYSTAL PALACE**, MANAGED **FULHAM** AND HAS HAD THREE SPELLS AS ASSISTANT MANAGER OF **WALES**.

**3** **"THE LEAP"** SCORED GOALS FOR **WALES, BOLTON WANDERERS, NEWCASTLE UNITED, STOCKPORT COUNTY** AND MORE AND PLAYED FOR BOTH MANCHESTER TEAMS IN THE '70S.

**4** STORIED STRIKER WHO MANAGED **WALES** AND **CITY**.

**5** WINGER WHO SPENT 11 YEARS WITH **CITY**, PLAYING IN TWO FA CUP FINALS, BEFORE JOINING **STOCKPORT COUNTY**, HE LATER MANAGED THE CITY SOCIAL CLUB FOR 25 YEARS.

**6** **FULHAM'S** RECORD GOALSCORER, HE SPENT A YEAR WITH **CITY** IN 1985.

**7**   HE STARTED WORK AS A PIT PONY DRIVER AT THE AGE OF 12, SPENT EIGHT YEARS WORKING DOWN THE MINES, PLAYED FOR BOTH *CITY* AND *UNITED* AND EARNED 48 CAPS BETWEEN 1895 AND 1920.

**8**   LOYAL SERVANT TO *CITY* BETWEEN 1957 AND 1968, A LEFT-BACK WHO MADE 248 APPEARANCES FOR THE CLUB BEFORE BECOMING RIGHT-HAND MAN TO *ALAN OAKES* AT *CHESTER CITY* FOR MANY YEARS.

# DANGER MEN AT WORK

**BERT TRAUTMANN** SUSTAINED ONE OF THE MOST INFAMOUS INJURIES IN SOCCER HISTORY WHEN HE DIVED AT THE FEET OF **BIRMINGHAM CITY'S PETER MURPHY** IN THE 1956 FA CUP FINAL. THE GERMAN GOALKEEPER WAS KNOCKED UNCONSCIOUS BUT DESPITE AN INJURY TO HIS NECK, BRAVELY INSISTED ON PLAYING ON. THAT COURAGE WAS UNDERLINED WHEN, DAYS LATER, HE FINALLY VISITED THE HOSPITAL AND AN X-RAY REVEALED HE HAD DISLOCATED FIVE VERTEBRAE, THE SECOND OF WHICH WAS CRACKED IN TWO! HE WAS FITTED WITH A SPECIAL BRACE AND SPENT MONTHS IN CONVALESCENCE.

**1** WHICH **CITY** GOALKEEPER'S CAREER INJURIES INCLUDED REPORTEDLY PULLING A MUSCLE IN HIS BACK WHEN REACHING FOR THE TV REMOTE CONTROL AND PULLING HIS SHOULDER WHILE FISHING?

**2** AFTER SUFFERING A SERIOUS THIGH INJURY IN WHAT WOULD PROVE TO BE HIS LAST GAME FOR **CITY** -- AFTER WHICH ONLY THE QUICK ACTION OF DOCTORS PREVENTED A BLOOD CLOT TURNING INTO SOMETHING MORE SERIOUS -- WHICH GOALKEEPER'S CAREER WAS ENDED WHEN HE SUFFERED MULTIPLE FRACTURES OF HIS RIGHT LEG WHILE PLAYING FOR **SUNDERLAND** IN 1996?

**3** WHICH **CITY** GOALKEEPER WAS HOSPITALISED AFTER SUFFERING CHEMICAL BURNS CAUSED BY DIVING ON THE **CARMARTHEN TOWN** PITCH WHILE PLAYING FOR **BARRY TOWN?**

**4** NAME THE **CITY** GOALKEEPER WHO, HAVING BROKEN A FINGER DURING A 1964 HOME GAME AGAINST **BURY**, MOVED TO CENTRE-FORWARD AND SCORED AN EQUALISING GOAL.

**5** **LIVERPOOL'S SADIO MANE** WAS SENT OFF FOR A 2017 CHALLENGE THAT LEFT WHICH CITY GOALKEEPER REQUIRING FACIAL STITCHES?

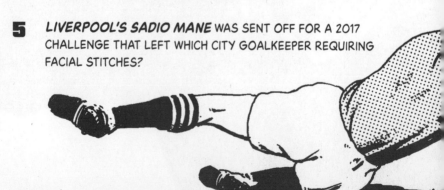

**6** WHOSE DAMAGED ACHILLES TENDON IN 2018 CAUSED AN INJURY CRISIS THAT NECESSITATED THE RECALL OF YOUNG GOALKEEPER *ARO MURIC* FROM *NAC BREDA?*

**7** WHICH *CITY* BACK-UP GOALKEEPER, WHO JOINED THE COACHING STAFF IN 2016, INJURED HIMSELF DURING HIS *EVERTON* DAYS WHEN HE FELL OFF A LADDER WHILE PUTTING HIS HOLIDAY SUITCASES IN THE LOFT ... AND TWO SEASONS LATER, DURING THE WARM UPS, TRIPPED OVER A WARNING SIGN ON THE PITCH AT *CHELSEA* AND INJURED HIS ANKLE?

**8** WHICH FORMER *CITY* GREAT WAS FORCED INTO RETIREMENT IN 1985 AFTER INJURING HIS NECK WHILE PLAYING ON THE ARTIFICIAL SURFACE AT *QUEENS PARK RANGERS?*

**9** WHILE PLAYING FOR *TORINO* AGAINST *AC MILAN* IN 2017, WHICH FORMER *CITY* GREAT SUFFERED A BRUTAL HEAD INJURY THAT LEFT HIM BLOODIED AND SWATHED IN BANDAGES AS HE PLAYED ON?

# MADRIDISTAS Y COLCHONEROS

ALTHOUGH *CITY* HAVE BEEN DRAWN THREE TIMES AGAINST *REAL MADRID* IN UEFA CHAMPIONS LEAGUE COMPETITION -- THE SIX GAMES PRODUCING TWO WINS, TWO DRAWS AND TWO LOSSES -- THEY HAVE YET TO MEET *REAL'S* CROSSTOWN RIVALS *ATLÉTICO DE MADRID*. HOWEVER, *CITY* HAVE DONE A FAIR AMOUNT OF TRANSFER BUSINESS INVOLVING *"MADRIDISTAS"* AND *"COLCHONEROS"*.

**1** WHILE ON LOAN AT *REAL MADRID* FROM *CITY* IN 2011, *EMMANUEL ADEBAYOR* WON THE COPA DEL REY -- ON HIS RETURN, HE WAS THEN LOANED OUT TO WHICH ENGLISH CLUB?

**2** *SERGIO AGÜERO* WON THE DON BALÓN, THE GOLDEN BOY, AND THE WORLD SOCCER YOUNG PLAYER OF THE YEAR AWARDS DURING HIS TIME WITH *ATLÉTICO MADRID*, AS WELL AS THE UEFA EUROPA LEAGUE AND THE UEFA SUPER CUP BEFORE JOINING *CITY* IN 2011 -- WHICH *CITY* SHIRT NUMBER DID HE TAKE ON HIS ARRIVAL?

**3** WHICH *ARGENTINA* INTERNATIONAL CENTRAL DEFENDER JOINED HIS FORMER *MÁLAGA* BOSS *MANUEL PELLEGRINI* AT *CITY* IN A £4.3 MILLION TRANSFER FROM *ATLÉTICO MADRID* IN 2013?

**4** WHO WON BOTH DOMESTIC CUPS WITH *LIVERPOOL* AND TWO UEFA CHAMPIONS LEAGUES, TWO LA LIGAS AND MORE WITH *REAL MADRID*, BEFORE JOINING *CITY* IN 2003?

**5** WHICH CONGOLESE-BORN, NATURALISED DUTCH WINGER ARRIVED ON LOAN FROM *ATLÉTICO MADRID* IN 2005 AND SCORED AGAINST *LIVERPOOL* TO GIVE *STUART PEARCE* HIS FIRST WIN AS MANAGER OF *CITY?*

**6** WHICH *CITY* PLAYER SCORED IN BOTH LEGS OF THE ROUND OF 16 GAMES AGAINST *REAL MADRID* IN THE 2020 UEFA CHAMPIONS LEAGUE COMPETITION?

**7** SIGNED TO *CITY* FROM *REAL MADRID* IN 2017, WHICH *BRAZIL* FULL-BACK LEFT FOR *JUVENTUS* IN 2019?

**8** NAME THE DEFENSIVE MIDFIELDER, A *SPAIN* INTERNATIONAL, SIGNED TO *CITY* FROM *ATLÉTICO MADRID* IN 2019 IN A RECORD £62.6 MILLION DEAL?

**9** WHO MANAGED BOTH *REAL MADRID* AND *CITY?*

**10** NAME THE BULGARIAN WINGER WHO JOINED *CITY* FROM *ATLÉTICO MADRID* IN A £4.7 MILLION DEAL IN 2007.

# MONACO MEN

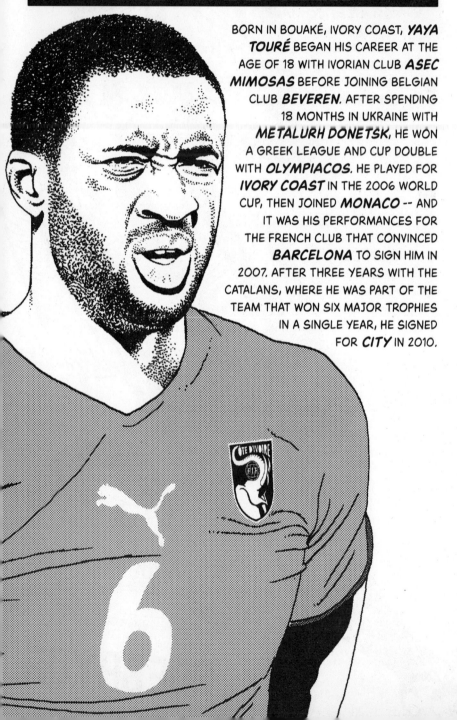

BORN IN BOUAKÉ, IVORY COAST, *YAYA TOURÉ* BEGAN HIS CAREER AT THE AGE OF 18 WITH IVORIAN CLUB *ASEC MIMOSAS* BEFORE JOINING BELGIAN CLUB *BEVEREN*. AFTER SPENDING 18 MONTHS IN UKRAINE WITH *METALURH DONETSK*, HE WON A GREEK LEAGUE AND CUP DOUBLE WITH *OLYMPIACOS*. HE PLAYED FOR *IVORY COAST* IN THE 2006 WORLD CUP, THEN JOINED *MONACO* -- AND IT WAS HIS PERFORMANCES FOR THE FRENCH CLUB THAT CONVINCED *BARCELONA* TO SIGN HIM IN 2007. AFTER THREE YEARS WITH THE CATALANS, WHERE HE WAS PART OF THE TEAM THAT WON SIX MAJOR TROPHIES IN A SINGLE YEAR, HE SIGNED FOR *CITY* IN 2010.

**1**   WHICH *FRANCE* FULL-BACK PLAYED FOR *LE HAVRE* AND *MARSEILLE* AND WON LIGUE 1 WITH *MONACO* BEFORE JOINING *CITY* IN 2017?

**2**   CAPPED 75 TIMES BY *BRAZIL*, WHICH RIGHT-BACK'S CLUBS INCLUDE *MONACO, INTERNAZIONALE, CITY* AND *ROMA*?

**3**   NAME THE ALGERIAN MIDFIELDER WHO PLAYED IN FRANCE WITH *MONACO, BORDEAUX* AND *PARIS SAINT-GERMAIN* BEFORE WINNING A FIRST DIVISION TITLE WITH *CITY* IN 2002.

**4**   WHICH TOGOLESE STRIKER REACHED A UEFA CHAMPIONS LEAGUE FINAL WITH *MONACO* AND JOINED *CITY* IN 2009?

**5**   NAME THE FORMER *MONACO* MIDFIELDER, WHOSE OTHER CLUBS INCLUDED *INTERNAZIONALE, PARMA, ATALANTA* AND *LAZIO*, WHOSE TRAINING GROUND BUST-UP WITH *JOEY BARTON* RESULTED IN ASSAULT CHARGES AGAINST THE *ENGLAND* MIDFIELDER.

**6**   NAME THE BALLON D'OR WINNER AND 1995 FIFA WORLD PLAYER OF THE YEAR WHO WON HONOURS WITH *MONACO, PARIS SAINT-GERMAIN, AC MILAN* AND *CHELSEA* AND SCORED FOUR GOALS DURING HIS BRIEF ELEVEN-GAME SPELL WITH *CITY*.

**7**   WHICH PORTUGUESE MIDFIELDER WON HONOURS WITH *BENFICA* AND *MONACO* AND MULTIPLE HONOURS WITH *CITY*, INCLUDING BEING NAMED THE 2019 *MANCHESTER CITY* PLAYER OF THE YEAR?

**8**   BORN IN BRAZIL, WHICH PORTUGUESE INTERNATIONAL CAME THROUGH THE RANKS AT *CITY*, JOINED *MONACO* FOR £9 MILLION IN 2015, PLAYED AT *LILLE* ON LOAN AND MOVED TO *SEVILLA* IN 2019?

# THE "NUTTER WITH THE PUTTER" AFFAIR!

OUTSIDE FOOTBALL, HIS CHARITABLE WORK IS EXTENSIVE AND EXEMPLARY -- BUT AS A PLAYER, CONTROVERSY AND *CRAIG BELLAMY* WENT HAND-IN-HAND. *BOBBY ROBSON* CALLED HIM "THE GOBBIEST FOOTBALLER I'VE EVER MET" AND BUST-UPS AND DUST-UPS WERE FREQUENT. FOLLOWING AN ARGUMENT IN TRAINING DURING A 2007 *LIVERPOOL* TRIP TO PORTUGAL, *BELLAMY* ASSAULTED A SLEEPING *JOHN ARNE RIISE* WITH A GOLF CLUB, EARNING HIMSELF A CLUB FINE OF TWO WEEKS' WAGES AND THE NICKNAME *"THE NUTTER WITH THE PUTTER"* FROM THE TABLOIDS!

AT WHICH CLUB DID *BELLAMY* PLAY UNDER:

**1** *MIKE WALKER, BRUCE RIOCH, BRYAN HAMILTON*

**2** *GORDON STRACHAN*

**3** *SIR BOBBY ROBSON, GRAEME SOUNESS*

**4** *MARTIN O'NEILL*

**5** *MARK HUGHES*

**6** *RAFA BENÍTEZ, SIR KENNY DALGLISH*

**7** *ALAN CURBISHLEY, GIANFRANCO ZOLA*

**8** *MARK HUGHES, ROBERTO MANCINI*

**9** *DAVE JONES, MALKY MACKAY, OLE GUNNAR SOLSKJAER*

# BETWEEN THE STICKS

LOCAL LAD *ALEX WILLIAMS* PROGRESSED THROUGH THE RANKS AT *CITY* TO BECOME *JOE CORRIGAN'S* SUCCESSOR -- BUT A RECURRING BACK INJURY FORCED HIS RETIREMENT IN 1987 AT THE AGE OF 26. FOR HIS WORK WITH YOUNG PEOPLE ON BEHALF OF *CITY IN THE COMMUNITY*, HE WAS AWARDED THE MBE IN THE 2002 NEW YEARS HONOURS LIST.

**1**   WHICH FULL-BACK WENT IN GOAL FOR *CITY* AFTER *CLAUDIO BRAVO* WAS INJURED IN A UEFA CHAMPIONS LEAGUE GAME AGAINST *ATALANTA* IN 2019?

**2**   NAME THE *MANCHESTER CITY* GOALKEEPER WHO WAS THE SECOND PLAYER INDUCTED INTO *WATFORD'S* HALL OF FAME, BEHIND CLUB LEGEND *LUTHER BLISSETT*.

**3**   IN 2019, WHICH FORMER *CITY* GOALKEEPER APPEARED AS A CONTESTANT ON TV'S *"STRICTLY COME DANCING"*, PAIRED WITH UKRAINIAN BALLROOM DANCER *NADIA BYCHKOVA?*

**4**   PRIOR TO SIGNING FOR *CITY* IN 1995, WHICH *WEST GERMANY* INTERNATIONAL GOALKEEPER SET THE BUNDESLIGA RECORD FOR MOST GOALS CONCEDED, LETTING IN 829 GOALS IN 534 GAMES?

**5**   WHICH FORMER *CITY* GOALKEEPER WAS APPOINTED CAPTAIN OF *THE FAROE ISLANDS* IN 2016?

**6**   WHO KEPT GOAL FOR *CITY* IN THE 2014 FOOTBALL LEAGUE CUP FINAL WHICH RESULTED IN A 3-1 VICTORY OVER *SUNDERLAND?*

**7**   NAME THE VETERAN *CITY* GOALKEEPER WHOSE CAREER SPANNED 29 CLUBS AND WHO ONCE TURNED OUT FOR *WOLVES* DRESSED IN A *SUPERMAN* OUTFIT?

**8**   IN A GAME AGAINST *SUNDERLAND* AT ROKER PARK IN 1900, *CITY'S CHARLIE WILLIAMS* ACHIEVED WHICH GOALKEEPING FIRST?

**9**   WHEN *JOE CORRIGAN* DISLOCATED HIS SHOULDER AFTER THREE MINUTES OF A 1982 GAME AGAINST *WATFORD*, WHICH FULL BACK WENT IN GOAL AND PULLED OFF A STRING OF SAVES IN A 1-0 WIN?

**10** WHICH *CITY* GOALKEEPER, CAPPED 31 TIMES BY *NORTHERN IRELAND* BETWEEN 1989 AND 1999, PURSUED A MANAGEMENT CAREER AND STEERED *ST. JOHNSTONE* TO VICTORY IN THE 2014 SCOTTISH CUP FINAL, THE FIRST MAJOR TROPHY IN THE CLUB'S HISTORY?

# 2018 WORLD CUP

VINCENT KOMPANY CAPTAINED BELGIUM TO THIRD PLACE IN THE 2014 WORLD CUP, THE COUNTRY'S HIGHEST-EVER PLACING IN THE TOURNAMENT. BELGIUM LOST TO EVENTUAL CHAMPIONS FRANCE IN THE SEMI-FINALS, AND BEAT ENGLAND IN THE THIRD PLACE PLAY-OFF GAME.

**1** *VINCENT KOMPANY* AND *KEVIN DE BRUYNE* WERE THE TWO *CITY* PLAYERS IN THE *BELGIUM* SQUAD, ALONG WITH WHICH FORMER *CITY* PLAYER THEN ON THE BOOKS AT *CELTIC?*

**2** *ENGLAND'S* SQUAD CONTAINED FOUR *CITY* PLAYERS -- *KYLE WALKER, JOHN STONES, RAHEEM STERLING* AND *FABIAN DELPH.* WHICH ONE SCORED TWICE DURING THE TOURNAMENT?

**3** *AUSTRALIA'S* SQUAD INCLUDED WHICH PLAYER WHO HAD SPENT HIS ENTIRE *CITY* CAREER ON LOAN AT *HUDDERSFIELD TOWN?*

**4** WHICH FORMER *CITY* PLAYER CAPTAINED THE *SERBIA* TEAM AND SCORED A GOAL AGAINST *COSTA RICA?*

**5** *BELGIUM* BEAT *BRAZIL* 2-1 IN THE QUARTER-FINAL ... WHICH TWO *CITY* PLAYERS GOT ON THE SCORESHEET?

**6** *SERGIO AGÜERO* -- WHO SCORED TWICE -- WAS IN THE *ARGENTINA* SQUAD, ALONG WITH *CITY* TEAMMATE *NICOLÁS OTAMENDI* AND WHICH FORMER *CITY* GOALKEEPER?

**7** WHICH FORMER *CITY* PLAYER WAS IN THE *DENMARK* SQUAD?

**8** *KELECHI IHEANACHO* REPRESENTED WHICH COUNTRY?

**9** WHO WAS THE ONLY *CITY* PLAYER IN THE *FRANCE* SQUAD?

**10** WHO WAS THE ONLY FORMER *CITY* PLAYER TO COACH A TEAM AT THE 2018 WORLD CUP?

# ARSENAL CONNECTIONS

TOMMY CATON MADE HIS SENIOR MANCHESTER CITY DEBUT AT THE AGE OF 16 AND PLAYED 100 GAMES FOR THE CLUB BEFORE HIS 20TH BIRTHDAY. CITY DROPPING DOWN A TIER IN 1983 PROMPTED CATON'S MOVE TO ARSENAL, WHERE HE WAS A REGULAR UNDER DON HOWE. HE FELL OUT OF FAVOUR UNDER SUBSEQUENT MANAGER GEORGE GRAHAM AND WAS TRANSFERRED TO OXFORD UNITED IN 1987, BEFORE JOINING CHARLTON ATHLETIC A YEAR LATER. A MONTH AFTER ANNOUNCING HIS RETIREMENT IN 1993, THE 30-YEAR-OLD -- WHO HAD LONG BATTLED ALCOHOL PROBLEMS -- DIED OF A HEART ATTACK.

IDENTIFY THESE PLAYERS WHOSE CLUBS INCLUDE CITY AND ARSENAL:

**1** FULL-BACK SIGNED FROM ARSENAL IN 1964. HE PLAYED 44 GAMES IN HIS DEBUT SEASON THAT SAW CITY PROMOTED TO THE TOP TIER. HE SUBSEQUENTLY JOINED READING BEFORE PLAYING AND MANAGING EXTENSIVELY IN IRISH FOOTBALL.

**2** VETERAN GOALKEEPER SIGNED BY KEVIN KEEGAN FROM ARSENAL IN 2003, HE PLAYED 26 GAMES FOR CITY THEN RETIRED.

**3** CAPPED 65 TIMES BY FRANCE, FULL-BACK WHO JOINED CITY ON A FREE TRANSFER WEEKS AFTER WINNING THE 2014 FA CUP WITH "THE GUNNERS". HE SUBSEQUENTLY SIGNED FOR ITALY'S BENEVENTO.

**4** HE WON THE 1968 EUROPEAN CUP WITH MANCHESTER UNITED BEFORE PLAYING FOR ARSENAL, CITY, EVERTON, BOLTON WANDERERS AND FORT LAUDERDALE STRIKERS.

**5** REPUBLIC OF IRELAND WINGER WHO WON HONOURS WITH NORTHAMPTON TOWN, CRYSTAL PALACE -- WHERE HE WAS VOTED PLAYER OF THE YEAR -- AND ARSENAL, HE JOINED CITY IN 1996 AND LATER PLAYED BRIEFLY FOR STOCKPORT COUNTY.

**6** ALAN BALL'S FINAL CITY SIGNING, HE JOINED FROM ARSENAL IN 1996 AND SEALED HIS PLACE IN CITY LEGEND WITH HIS INJURY TIME EQUALISER IN THE PROMOTION PLAY-OFF AGAINST GILLINGHAM THAT SET UP CITY'S RETURN TO THE SECOND TIER.

**7** CAPPED 20 TIMES BY *FRANCE*, FULL-BACK WHO WON LEAGUE
TITLES WITH *ARSENAL*, *CITY* AND *İSTANBUL BAŞAKŞEHIR*.

# "BRAVEHEARTS"

A TOUGH, NO-NONSENSE DEFENDER FROM THE SCOTTISH HIGHLANDS, WHO PLAYED OVER 600 GAMES DURING HIS CAREER, *COLIN HENDRY* TURNED PROFESSIONAL WITH *DUNDEE* BEFORE HEADING SOUTH OF THE BORDER. HE WAS 27 YEARS OLD BEFORE HE EARNED THE FIRST OF HIS 51 *SCOTLAND* CAPS.

IDENTIFY THESE *CITY* PLAYERS WHO EARNED *SCOTLAND* CAPS:

**1** PLAYED FOR *HUDDERSFIELD TOWN*, *CITY*, *MANCHESTER UNITED* AND *TORINO*, HE SCORED 30 GOALS IN 55 APPEARANCES FOR *SCOTLAND*.

**2** HE WON THE 1934 FA CUP WITH *CITY*, PLAYED FOR *LIVERPOOL* AND MANAGED *MANCHESTER UNITED*.

**3** HIS CLUBS INCLUDED *ARSENAL*, *LUTON TOWN*, *BRIGHTON & HOVE ALBION*, *CITY*, *LEICESTER CITY*, *BLACKBURN ROVERS*, *CRYSTAL PALACE*, *BLACKPOOL*, *DERBY COUNTY*, *LEEDS UNITED* AND *OLDHAM ATHLETIC*.

**4** PLAYED FOR *WEST BROMWICH ALBION*, *CITY*, *NOTTINGHAM FOREST*, *EVERTON*, *FORT LAUDERDALE SUN*, *NORWICH CITY*, *BOLTON WANDERERS*, *STOCKPORT COUNTY*, *OLDHAM ATHLETIC* AND *SHREWSBURY TOWN*.

**5** HE PLAYED IN THE *"WEMBLEY WIZARDS"* *SCOTLAND* SIDE THAT THRASHED *ENGLAND* 5-1 AT WEMBLEY IN 1928, PLAYED FOR *CITY* 242 TIMES, INCLUDING IN THE 1926 AND 1933 FA CUP FINALS, AND MANAGED *OLDHAM ATHLETIC*, *ASTON VILLA*, *NOTTS COUNTY* AND *SHEFFIELD WEDNESDAY*.

**6** STRIKER WHO WON FOUR SCOTTISH LEAGUE TITLES, THREE SCOTTISH CUPS AND FOUR SCOTTISH LEAGUE CUPS WITH *RANGERS*, BEFORE WINNING PROMOTION WITH *CITY* IN 1966. HE WENT ON TO PLAY FOR *SUNDERLAND*, *RAITH ROVERS* AND *HAMILTON ACADEMICAL*.

# PORTUGUESE MEN O' CITY

IN 2018, **BRAZIL** GOALKEEPER **EDERSON** SET THE GUINNESS WORLD RECORD FOR LONGEST FOOTBALL DROP KICK WHEN HE LAUNCHED THE BALL AN INCREDIBLE 75.35 M (247 FT 2 IN) AT THE ETIHAD CAMPUS. AFTER LAUNCHING HIS CAREER IN HIS HOMELAND, HE WON TWO PORTUGUESE LEAGUE AND CUP DOUBLES WITH **BENFICA** BEFORE SIGNING FOR **CITY** IN 2017, WINNING A LEAGUE AND LEAGUE CUP DOUBLE IN HIS DEBUT SEASON. EARLY IN HIS SECOND SEASON, HE BECAME THE FIRST **CITY** GOALKEEPER TO PROVIDE A PREMIER LEAGUE ASSIST, WHEN HIS LENGTHY GOAL-KICK WAS CONVERTED BY **SERGIO AGÜERO** FOR THE OPENING GOAL IN A 6-1 VICTORY OVER **HUDDERSFIELD TOWN**.

WHICH PORTUGUESE CLUBS HAVE THE FOLLOWING PLAYED FOR?

**1** *NICOLÁS OTAMENDI* (TWO CLUBS)

**2** *RÚBEN DIAS*

**3** *BERNARDO SILVA*

**4** *FELIPE CAICEDO*

**5**    *DANILO*

**6**    *FERNANDO* (TWO CLUBS)

**7**    *JOÃO CANCELO*

**8**    *RONY LOPES*

**9**    *ELIAQUIM MANGALA*

# PSYCHO!

*ROY KEANE* DESCRIBED HIM AS *"A MAN AMONGST BOYS"* AND *MATT LE TISSIER* SAID HE WAS HIS SCARIEST OPPONENT. NICKNAMED *"PSYCHO"* FOR HIS UNCOMPROMISING, COMMITTED DEFENDING, *STUART PEARCE* -- WHO WAS *KEVIN KEEGAN'S* FIRST SIGNING AT *CITY* IN 2001 -- WAS CAPPED 78 TIMES BY *ENGLAND*.

**1** WHILE WORKING AS AN ELECTRICIAN, HE PLAYED FOR WHICH NON-LEAGUE TEAM -- THE SAME CLUB THAT ALSO LAUNCHED THE CAREERS OF *VINNIE JONES* AND *JERMAINE BECKFORD?*

**2** *PEARCE* WAS SIGNED TO WHICH TOP-FLIGHT CLUB IN 1983 BY MANAGER *BOBBY GOULD?*

**3** SIGNED TO *NOTTINGHAM FOREST* BY *BRIAN CLOUGH* IN 1985, *PEARCE* LATER PLAYED AT THE CLUB UNDER WHICH SUBSEQUENT *CITY* MANAGER?

**4** HE PLAYED IN THE 1998 FA CUP FINAL FOR WHICH TEAM MANAGED BY *KENNY DALGLISH?*

**5** *PEARCE* SPENT TWO SEASONS AT THE TURN OF THE MILLENNIUM PLAYING FOR *WEST HAM UNITED* UNDER WHICH MANAGER?

**6** WHO FOLLOWED *PEARCE* AS MANAGER OF *MANCHESTER CITY?*

**7** *PEARCE* WAS APPOINTED CARETAKER MANAGER OF *ENGLAND* IN 2012 FOLLOWING THE DEPARTURE OF WHICH MANAGER?

# SO LONG!

WHEN **DANIEL STURRIDGE** JOINED **CITY'S** ACADEMY AT THE AGE OF 13, AN FA TRIBUNAL ORDERED THE CLUB TO PAY £30,000 TO **COVENTRY CITY** IN COMPENSATION, WITH THE POTENTIAL OF RISING TO £200,000 WITH ADD-ONS. THE FOLLOWING YEAR, HE JUSTIFIED **CITY'S** FAITH WHEN HE WAS THE LEADING SCORER AND VOTED PLAYER OF THE TOURNAMENT -- A FEAT PREVIOUSLY ACHIEVED BY **CARLOS TEVEZ** -- AS **CITY** WON THE NIKE CUP, THE WORLD'S LARGEST UNDER-15 TOURNAMENT.

HE IMPRESSED IN HIS LIMITED APPEARANCES FOR THE FIRST TEAM AND THERE WERE HIGH HOPES FOR HIS PROGRESS AT **CITY** -- BUT WHEN HIS CONTRACT EXPIRED IN 2009, HE OPTED TO SIGN FOR **CHELSEA**. ONCE MORE, A TRIBUNAL WAS REQUIRED, AND A FEE OF £3.5 MILLION SET, WHICH EVENTUALLY ROSE TO £8.3 MILLION WHEN ADD-ONS WERE FACTORED IN.

WHICH CLUBS DID THE FOLLOWING LEAVE **CITY** TO JOIN IN THE SUMMER OF 2009?

1   **ELANO**

2   **GELSON FERNANDES**

3   **TAL BEN HAIM**

4   **DARIUS VASSELL**

5   **VALERI BOJINOV**

6   **KASPER SCHMEICHEL**

7   **RICHARD DUNNE**

8   **CHED EVANS**

9   **JOE HART**

10  **KELVIN ETUHU**

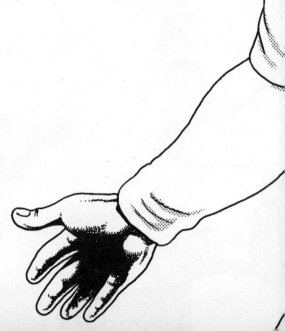

# ROBERTO'S RECRUITS

DURING **ROBERTO MANCINI'S** 30-MONTH TENURE AS MANAGER, **CITY** BROUGHT 21 NEW PLAYERS INTO THE CLUB, INCLUDING **DAVID SILVA**, **SERGIO AGÜERO**, **EDIN DŽEKO** AND **MARIO BALOTELLI**.

FROM WHICH TEAMS WERE THE FOLLOWING PLAYERS SIGNED?

**1**  *JACK RODWELL*

**2**  *JAVI GARCÍA*

**3**  *STEFAN SAVIĆ*

**4**  *MAICON*

**5**  *MATIJA NASTASIĆ*

**6**  *OWEN HARGREAVES*

7  ALEKSANDAR KOLAROV

8  RICHARD WRIGHT

9  SCOTT SINCLAIR

10  JÉRÔME BOATENG

11  JAMES MILNER

12  PATRICK VIEIRA

# EURO 2020 VISION

*JOHN STONES* CAME THROUGH THE RANKS AT HIS LOCAL CLUB, *BARNSLEY*, AND SIGNED FOR *EVERTON* IN A £3 MILLION DEAL WHEN HE WAS 18. HE MADE HIS *ENGLAND* DEBUT IN 2014, WAS VOTED *EVERTON* YOUNG PLAYER OF THE YEAR IN 2015, AND JOINED *CITY* IN 2016, THE CLUB PAYING AN INITIAL £47.5 MILLION PLUS £2.5 MILLION IN ADD-ONS.

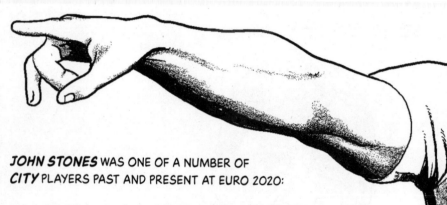

*JOHN STONES* WAS ONE OF A NUMBER OF *CITY* PLAYERS PAST AND PRESENT AT EURO 2020:

**1** NAME ONE OF THE THREE FORMER *CITY* ACADEMY PLAYERS INCLUDED IN THE *WALES* SQUAD -- A *CRYSTAL PALACE* GOALKEEPER, A *BOURNEMOUTH* MIDFIELDER AND A *CITY* MIDFIELDER ON LOAN AT *DONCASTER ROVERS*.

**2** WHICH *CITY* STAR WAS RULED OUT OF THE TOURNAMENT AFTER TESTING POSITIVE FOR COVID-19?

**3** NAME THE FOUR *CITY* PLAYERS PAST AND PRESENT WHO REPRESENTED *SPAIN*.

**4** *ENGLAND'S* SQUAD CONTAINED CURRENT *CITY* PLAYERS *STONES*, *KYLE WALKER*, *RAHEEM STERLING* AND *PHIL FODEN* AS WELL AS WHICH TWO PRODUCTS OF THE *CITY* YOUTH SYSTEM?

**5** HOW MANY PAST AND PRESENT *CITY* PLAYERS WERE INCLUDED IN THE *GERMANY* SQUAD?

**6** NAME THE TWO FORMER *CITY* PLAYERS INCLUDED ALONGSIDE *KEVIN DE BRUYNE* IN THE *BELGIUM* SQUAD.

**7** NAME THE TWO FORMER *CITY* PLAYERS IN THE *SLOVAKIA* SQUAD.

**8** *OLEKSANDR ZINCHENKO* SCORED A GOAL AND ASSISTED ON THE WINNER IN HIS STAR OF THE MATCH PERFORMANCE IN *UKRAINE'S* 2-1 VICTORY OVER WHICH NATION IN THE ROUND OF 16?

# PSYCHO'S SIGNINGS!

*EKA BASUNGA LOKONDA "ÉMILE" MPENZA* WAS BORN IN ZELLIK, BELGIUM, ON JULY 4, 1978. HE MADE HIS NAME AT *STANDARD LIEGE* ALONGSIDE OLDER BROTHER *MBO*, AND THE TWO WERE BOTH MEMBERS OF *BELGIUM'S* 1998 WORLD CUP SQUAD. *ÉMILE* JOINED *CITY* FROM *HAMBURGER SV* IN 2007, SIGNED BY *STUART PEARCE* TOWARDS THE END OF HIS TENURE, MOVING ON TO *PORTSMOUTH* IN 2008.

FROM WHICH CLUBS DID *STUART PEARCE* SIGN THESE PLAYERS?

**1** *DARIUS VASSELL*

**2** *JAVIER GARRIDO*

**3** *JOE HART*

**4** *DIETMAR HAMANN*

**5** *PAUL DICKOV*

**6** *HATEM TRABELSI*

**7** *ALBERT RIERA*

**8** *ANDREAS ISAKSSON*

**9** *OUSMANE DABO*

**10** *MICHAEL BALL*

# GERMAN EXPORTS

**NIGEL DE JONG** AND **VINCENT KOMPANY** WERE BOTH SIGNED FROM **HAMBURGER SV.** FROM WHICH GERMAN CLUB DID **CITY** ACQUIRE THE FOLLOWING PLAYERS?

1 LEROY SANÉ

2 ILKAY GÜNDOGAN

3 JÉRÔME BOATENG

4 MICHAEL TARNAT

5 DINO
TOPPMÖLLER

6 MICHAEL
FRONTZECK

7 EIKE IMMEL

8 MAURIZIO
GAUDINO

9 STEFFEN KARL

10 UWE RÖSLER

# THE "REVIE PLAN" MAN

DON REVIE ARRIVED AT *MAINE ROAD* IN 1951 IN A £25,000 TRANSFER FROM *HULL CITY*. THE SIDE STRUGGLED, UNTIL A TACTICAL INNOVATION -- BASED ON THE STYLE OF PLAY ADOPTED BY *HUNGARY'S "MAGICAL MAGYARS"* NATIONAL TEAM -- WHICH FEATURED *REVIE* AS A DEEP-LYING CENTRE-FORWARD, SAW THE TEAM REACH THE 1955 CUP FINAL AND *REVIE* NAMED FWA FOOTBALLER OF THE YEAR. ALTHOUGH THE TACTIC WAS DUBBED *"THE REVIE PLAN"*, IT HAD ORIGINALLY BEEN ADOPTED BY *CITY'S* RESERVE TEAM A YEAR EARLIER WHEN IT ALLOWED THEM TO GO UNBEATEN IN THE LAST 26 GAMES OF THE 1953-54 SEASON.

IN THE 29 GAMES THAT *REVIE* OVERSAW AS *ENGLAND* MANAGER IN THE 1970S, HE SELECTED FOUR PLAYERS WHO WOULD LATER MANAGE *CITY* -- *KEVIN KEEGAN, ALAN BALL, JOE ROYLE* AND *PHIL NEAL*.

HE ALSO SELECTED THE FOLLOWING PLAYERS WHO HAD PLAYED, OR WOULD PLAY, FOR *CITY*:

**1** CENTRE-HALF WHO WON THE 1973 FA CUP WITH *SUNDERLAND*.

**2** STRIKER WHO WON THE 1976 FA CUP WITH *SOUTHAMPTON* AND THE 1985 LEAGUE CUP WITH *NORWICH CITY*.

**3** FORMER *BURY* PLAYER WHO WON EVERY DOMESTIC HONOUR AND THE EUROPEAN CUP WINNERS' CUP WITH *CITY*.

**4** HE WON HONOURS WITH *SUNDERLAND, CITY* AND THE *NEW YORK COSMOS*.

**5** FORWARD WHO WON HONOURS WITH *IPSWICH TOWN* AND *LIVERPOOL*.

**6** TOUGH MIDFIELDER WHO WAS VOTED PLAYER OF THE YEAR AT BOTH *CITY* AND *STOKE CITY*.

**7** GOALKEEPER WHO WON TWO LEAGUE CUPS AND THE EUROPEAN CUP WINNERS' CUP WITH *CITY*.

**8** BRITAIN'S FIRST £1 MILLION PLAYER.

**9** EUROPEAN CUP WINNERS' CUP WINNER WITH *CITY* AND A MEMBER OF THE TEAM THAT LOST THE 1974 LEAGUE CUP FINAL, AFTER WHICH HE JOINED *SUNDERLAND*.

**10** RELEASED BY *CITY* IN 1970 AFTER CLASHING WITH *MALCOLM ALLISON*, MAVERICK PLAYER WHO SPENT SEVEN YEARS AT *QUEENS PARK RANGERS*.

# ANARCHIC ANELKA

**NICOLAS ANELKA** IS ANOTHER **CITY** ALUMNUS WHO ATTRACTED CONTROVERSY THROUGHOUT HIS CAREER. HE WAS ONCE BANNED FOR FIVE MATCHES BY THE FA AND FINED £80,000 AFTER MAKING AN OFFENSIVE HAND GESTURE, CALLED THE **"QUENELLE"**, THAT FRENCH AUTHORITIES HAVE SOUGHT TO BAN. HE WAS CAPPED 69 TIMES BY **FRANCE** BUT HIS INTERNATIONAL CAREER GROUND TO A HALT WHEN HE WAS EXPELLED FROM THE SQUAD AFTER INSULTING MANAGER **RAYMOND DOMENECH** AT HALF-TIME IN A 2010 WORLD CUP GAME AGAINST **MEXICO**.

**1** **ANELKA** BEGAN HIS CAREER AT WHICH FRENCH CLUB -- TO WHICH HE WOULD LATER RETURN?

**2** HE JOINED **ARSENAL** AS A 17-YEAR-OLD IN 1997, WINNING THE DOUBLE IN HIS SECOND SEASON. WHO DID **ARSENAL** DEFEAT IN THE 1998 FA CUP FINAL?

**3** **ANELKA** WON THE 2000 CHAMPIONS LEAGUE WITH WHICH TEAM?

**4** A LOAN SPELL AT **LIVERPOOL** ENDED WHEN **GÉRARD HOULLIER** OPTED TO SIGN WHICH **SENEGAL** FORWARD RATHER THAN OFFER **ANELKA** A PERMANENT DEAL?

**5** WHICH MANAGER PAID A CLUB RECORD £13 MILLION TO SIGN **ANELKA** TO **CITY** IN 2002?

**6** HE LEFT **CITY** FOR WHICH TURKISH TEAM, WITH WHOM HE WON THE 2005 SÜPER LIG?

**7** NAME TWO OF THE THREE MANAGERS HE PLAYED UNDER AT **BOLTON WANDERERS** BETWEEN AUGUST 2006 AND JANUARY 2008, WHEN HE LEFT FOR **CHELSEA**.

**8** HE WON THE PREMIER LEAGUE GOLDEN BOOT WITH **CHELSEA** IN 2009, THE SAME YEAR HE WAS JOINT FA CUP TOP SCORER WITH WHICH **ARSENAL** STRIKER? (**CHELSEA** WON THE FA CUP THAT SEASON AND THE DOUBLE THE NEXT).

**9** HE JOINED CHINA'S **SHANGHAI SHENHUA** IN 2012 BUT RETURNED TO WHICH ITALIAN CLUB ON LOAN TO WIN A SERIE A TITLE?

**10** HE RETURNED TO ENGLAND TO PLAY FOR WHICH TEAM, THE SIXTH AND FINAL PREMIER LEAGUE CLUB OF HIS CAREER?

**11** HIS FINAL CLUB WAS WHICH INDIAN SUPER LEAGUE TEAM?

# CALAMITY JAMES

WHEN A SPATE OF ERRORS EARNED HIM THE NICKNAME "CALAMITY JAMES" EARLY IN HIS CAREER, HE PUT HIS LACK OF CONCENTRATION DOWN TO AN OVERINDULGENCE IN VIDEO GAMES. CAPPED 53 TIMES BY **ENGLAND**, **DAVID JAMES** WAS RENOWNED FOR HIS EXTRA-CURRICULAR ACTIVITIES. A 20-A-DAY SMOKER EARLY IN HIS CAREER, HE LATER FRONTED AN ANTI-SMOKING CAMPAIGN. A MODEL WITH BRANDS SUCH AS **GIORGIO ARMANI** AND **H&M**, HE IS ALSO A CHILDREN'S BOOK ILLUSTRATOR.

**1** JAMES BEGAN HIS CAREER WITH WHICH SECOND-TIER CLUB?

**2** WITH WHICH CLUB DID HE WIN THE 1995 LEAGUE CUP?

**3** HE PLAYED IN WHICH TEAM'S LOSS TO **CHELSEA** IN THE 2000 FA CUP FINAL, THE LAST TO BE STAGED AT THE OLD WEMBLEY?

**4** HE JOINED **CITY** IN 2004 AFTER BEING RELEGATED WITH WHICH LONDON CLUB?

**5** HE SIGNED TO **CITY** AS A REPLACEMENT FOR WHICH OTHER **ENGLAND** INTERNATIONAL GOALKEEPER?

**6** HE EARNED AN FA CUP FINAL-WINNER'S MEDAL WITH **PORTSMOUTH** IN 2008 WITH THE 1-0 VICTORY OVER WHICH TEAM?

**7** HE CAPTAINED **PORTSMOUTH** IN AN FA CUP FINAL DEFEAT AGAINST WHICH TEAM IN 2010, BECOMING THE OLDEST GOALKEEPER TO APPEAR IN AN FA CUP FINAL?

**8** **JAMES** SET A PREMIER LEAGUE RECORD OF 169 CLEAN SHEETS THAT WAS SURPASSED BY WHICH GOALKEEPER IN 2015?

**9** NAME TWO OF THE FOUR MANAGERS UNDER WHOM HE PLAYED AT **PORTSMOUTH** BETWEEN AUGUST 2006 AND THE SUMMER OF 2010.

**10** IN 2010, HE SIGNED FOR WHICH WEST COUNTRY CLUB NICKNAMED **"THE ROBINS"**?

**11** HE SUBSEQUENTLY PLAYED A FEW MONTHS UNDER *EDDIE HOWE* AT WHICH CLUB?

**12** IN 2013, HE PLAYED FOR *ÍBV VESTMANNAEYJAR* -- IN WHICH COUNTRY IS THAT CLUB BASED?

**13** HE MANAGED *KERALA BLASTERS* -- A CLUB BASED IN WHICH COUNTRY?

# MAKE 'EM MACKEMS

HAVING EXPERIENCED RELEGATION WITH **SUNDERLAND, DENNIS TUEART** TASTED GLORY AS A MEMBER OF THE CLUB'S 1973 FA CUP-WINNING TEAM. HE BEGAN THE FIRST OF HIS TWO SPELLS WITH **CITY** IN 1974, RETURNING TO THE CLUB IN 1980 AFTER PLAYING WITH THE **NEW YORK COSMOS.**

IDENTIFY THESE **CITY** PLAYERS WHO ALSO PLAYED FOR **SUNDERLAND:**

**1** BELGIUM INTERNATIONAL WHO WAS LOANED OUT FROM **CITY** TO **CELTIC, SUNDERLAND** AND **GALATASARAY** BEFORE A PERMANENT TRANSFER TO **LYON** IN 2018.

**2** ISRAEL INTERNATIONAL DEFENDER LOANED OUT TO **SUNDERLAND** FROM **CITY** IN 2009 BEFORE SIGNING FOR **PORTSMOUTH.**

**3** AFTER A LOAN SPELL WITH **SUNDERLAND,** HE JOINED **QUEENS PARK RANGERS** AND WAS PART OF THE DEFENCE THAT FACED **CITY** ON THE TITLE-WINNING FINAL DAY OF THE 2012 SEASON.

**4** MADE 41 APPEARANCES FOR THE **ZIMBABWE** NATIONAL TEAM.

**5** MIDFIELDER WHO PLAYED IN THE 1974 LEAGUE CUP FINAL BEFORE JOINING **SUNDERLAND** IN THE EXCHANGE DEAL INVOLVING **DENNIS TUEART,** HE WAS CAPPED THREE TIMES BY **ENGLAND** AND LATER PLAYED FOR **BIRMINGHAM CITY.**

**6** ARRIVED AT **CITY** FROM **SUNDERLAND** IN 1974 AS PART OF THE PACKAGE DEAL THAT BROUGHT **TUEART** TO THE CLUB, HIS SUBSEQUENT CLUBS INCLUDED **PLYMOUTH ARGYLE, HULL CITY** AND **CARLISLE UNITED.**

**7** ENGLAND INTERNATIONAL WHO WON THE 1956 FA CUP WITH **CITY** BEFORE JOINING **SUNDERLAND** AND THEN LAUNCHING HIS MANAGEMENT CAREER WITH **LEEDS UNITED.**

**8** HUNGARY INTERNATIONAL GOALKEEPER, HE JOINED **CITY** ON LOAN FROM **SUNDERLAND** IN 2010, BEFORE MOVING ON TO **IPSWICH TOWN.** SADLY, HE DIED OF CANCER IN 2015, AGED 32.

**9** **ENGLAND** DEFENDER WHO WON HONOURS WITH **CHELSEA**, HE WAS LOANED OUT TO **WEST HAM UNITED**, **SUNDERLAND** AND **BRIGHTON & HOVE ALBION** FROM **CITY** BEFORE JOINING R**EADING** IN 2013.

**10** HOT YOUNG PROSPECT AT **EVERTON**, WHERE HE GAINED HIS FIRST **ENGLAND** CAPS, HE JOINED **CITY** IN 2014 BUT HIS CAREER STALLED BADLY, LEADING TO DISAPPOINTING SPELLS WITH **SUNDERLAND**, **BLACKBURN ROVERS** AND **SHEFFIELD UNITED**.

# THE MAN WITH ONE NAME

ALTHOUGH HE HAD WON SIX LEAGUE TITLES, FOUR UKRAINIAN CUPS, TWO UKRAINIAN SUPER CUPS AND THE UEFA CUP WITH **SHAKHTAR DONETSK**, **FERNANDINHO** -- REAL NAME **FERNANDO LUIZ ROZA** -- WAS SO INTENT ON JOINING **CITY** IN 2013 THAT, TO GET THE DEAL OVER THE LINE, HE REPORTEDLY WAIVED £4 MILLION OWED TO HIM BY **SHAKHTAR**.

IDENTIFY THESE OTHER **CITY** PLAYERS KNOWN BY A SINGLE NAME:

**1**   *RODRIGO HERNÁNDEZ CASCANTE*

**2**   *JOSÉ ÁNGEL ESMORÍS TASENDE*

**3**   FULL-BACK SIGNED FROM **INTERNAZIONALE** IN 2012.

**4**   *MANUEL AGUDO DURÁN*

**5**   MIDFIELDER SIGNED FROM **SHAKHTAR DONETSK** IN 2007

**6**   *SYLVIO MENDES CAMPOS JÚNIOR*

**7**   BRAZILIAN MIDFIELDER WHO WON THE 2016 LEAGUE CUP WITH **CITY**.

**8**   *JOÃO ALVES DE ASSIS SILVA*

**9**   **BRAZIL** MIDFIELDER WHO, AFTER LEAVING **CITY** IN 2008, SCORED **HULL CITY'S** FIRST EVER PREMIER LEAGUE GOAL.

**10**   BRAZILIAN WHO BECAME A CULT HERO AT **CITY**. AFTER BEING AN UNUSED SUBSTITUTE 20 TIMES, HE CAME ON IN THE 84TH MINUTE AGAINST **BOLTON WANDERERS** ON THE FINAL DAY OF THE 2008-09 SEASON TO A RAPTUROUS RECEPTION, RECEIVING A STANDING OVATION WHEN HE TOOK A THROW-IN.

# IT'S A FAMILY AFFAIR

*PETER SCHMEICHEL* WAS BORN IN GLADSAXE, ON NOVEMBER 18, 1963. THREE TIMES DANISH FOOTBALLER OF THE YEAR, HE WON THREE LEAGUE TITLES WITH *BRØNDBY*, BEFORE JOINING *MANCHESTER UNITED* IN 1991. HE WON FIVE LEAGUE TITLES WITH *"THE RED DEVILS"*, INCLUDING TWO LEAGUE AND FA CUP DOUBLES, AND A UNIQUE TREBLE OF ENGLISH LEAGUE, FA CUP AND UEFA CHAMPIONS LEAGUE IN 1999. HE MOVED ON TO *SPORTING CP* AND WON A LEAGUE TITLE IN HIS DEBUT SEASON, BEFORE RETURNING TO ENGLISH FOOTBALL WITH *ASTON VILLA* AND *CITY*. HIS GOALKEEPER SON, *KASPER SCHMEICHEL*, HAS FOLLOWED IN HIS FOOTSTEPS. AFTER LAUNCHING HIS CAREER AT *CITY*, HE HAS WON PREMIER LEAGUE AND FA CUP HONOURS WITH *LEICESTER CITY*, REPRESENTED *DENMARK* AT INTERNATIONAL LEVEL, AND WON MULTIPLE DANISH FOOTBALLER OF THE YEAR AWARDS.

NAME THESE RELATIVES WHO HAVE REPRESENTED *CITY:*

**1** FATHER *MIKE* AND SON *NICKY* WHO BOTH LAUNCHED THEIR CAREERS AT *SWINDON TOWN.*

**2** TWIN BROTHERS WHO JOINED *CITY* FROM *LUTON TOWN* IN 1978.

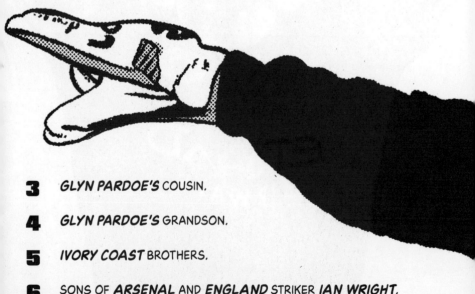

**3** *GLYN PARDOE'S* COUSIN.

**4** *GLYN PARDOE'S* GRANDSON.

**5** *IVORY COAST* BROTHERS.

**6** SONS OF *ARSENAL* AND *ENGLAND* STRIKER *IAN WRIGHT.*

**7**   SON WHO PLAYED UNDER MANAGER DAD *JOHN* IN THE EARLY 1980S.

**8**   SONS OF OLYMPIC 800M GOLD MEDAL WINNER *ANN PACKER*, THEY BOTH WON HONOURS WITH *CITY* IN THE MID-1980S.

**9**   FA CUP-WINNING DAD *KEN* AND LEAGUE CUP-WINNING SON *PETER*.

**10**   SON OF THE *ENGLAND* STRIKER WHO WON THE 1999 UEFA CHAMPIONS LEAGUE WITH *MANCHESTER UNITED*.

**11**   GERMAN-BORN BROTHERS *LUKAS* AND *FELIX*.

**12**   ZAMBIAN-BORN BROTHERS *JIM* AND *JEFF*.

**13**   DAD OF *FILIPPO* AND *ANDREA* OF *CITY'S* UNDER-21 YOUTH TEAM.

# PALACE INTRIGUE

AFTER TWO SPELLS IN CHARGE OF **CRYSTAL PALACE**, FORMER **MANCHESTER UNITED** WINGER **STEVE COPPELL** WAS INSTALLED AS **CITY** MANAGER IN OCTOBER, 1996. IN A MOVE THAT SENT SHOCKWAVES THROUGH MANCHESTER, HE QUIT AFTER ONLY SIX GAMES AND 33 DAYS IN CHARGE! HE WOULD GO ON TO MANAGE **CRYSTAL PALACE** TWICE MORE, AND TAKE THE REINS AT A NUMBER OF CLUBS, INCLUDING **BRENTFORD, BRIGHTON & HOVE ALBION, READING** AND **BRISTOL CITY**.

IDENTIFY THESE **CITY** BOSSES BY THE OTHER CLUBS THEY MANAGED:

**1** *FIORENTINA, LAZIO, INTER MILAN, GALATASARAY, INTER MILAN, ZENIT SAINT PETERSBURG*

**2** *PHILADELPHIA FURY, BLACKPOOL, PORTSMOUTH, STOKE CITY, EXETER CITY, SOUTHAMPTON, PORTSMOUTH*

**3** *BATH CITY, TORONTO CITY, PLYMOUTH ARGYLE, CRYSTAL PALACE, GALATASARAY, YEOVIL TOWN, SPORTING CP, MIDDLESBROUGH, WILLINGTON, VITÓRIA DE SETÚBAL, SC FARENSE, FISHER ATHLETIC, BRISTOL ROVERS*

**4** *BLACKBURN ROVERS, EVERTON, ATHLETIC BILBAO, XANTHI, NOTTS COUNTY, SHEFFIELD UNITED, ETHNIKOS PIRAEUS*

**5** *DEGERFORS IF, IFK GÖTEBORG, BENFICA, ROMA, FIORENTINA, SAMPDORIA, LAZIO, LEICESTER CITY, GUANGZHOU R&F, SHANGHAI SIPG, SHENZHEN*

**6** *BLACKBURN ROVERS, FULHAM, QUEENS PARK RANGERS, STOKE CITY, SOUTHAMPTON*

**7** *OLDHAM ATHLETIC, EVERTON, IPSWICH TOWN*

**8** *HULL CITY, OXFORD UNITED, HUDDERSFIELD, BRIGHTON & HOVE ALBION, PORT VALE, MACCLESFIELD TOWN*

**9** *SUNDERLAND, LEEDS UNITED, COVENTRY CITY, PLYMOUTH ARGYLE, MUMBAI CITY*

# SENT TO COVENTRY

HAVING WON PROMOTION AND A LEAGUE CUP WINNERS' MEDAL WITH **ASTON VILLA**, SCOTTISH LEFT-BACK **BOBBY MCDONALD** SPENT FIVE YEARS AT **COVENTRY CITY** BEFORE JOINING **CITY** IN 1980. HE PLAYED IN THE FA CUP IN HIS DEBUT SEASON AND IN 1983 JOINED **OXFORD UNITED**, WITH WHOM HE WON TWO PROMOTIONS IN THREE SEASONS. AFTER PLAYING FOR **LEEDS UNITED** AND **WOLVERHAMPTON WANDERERS**, HE PLAYED IN NON-LEAGUE FOOTBALL IN THE TWILIGHT OF HIS CAREER.

**1** WHICH FORMER **MANCHESTER CITY** BOSS MANAGED **COVENTRY CITY** BETWEEN 1972 AND 1974?

**2** WHICH **CITY** GOALKEEPER WAS LOANED OUT TO **COVENTRY CITY** BEFORE JOINING **NOTTS COUNTY** IN 2009?

**3** NAME THE IRISH MIDFIELDER WHO WAS LOANED OUT BY **CITY** TO **COVENTRY CITY** AND **ROCHDALE** BEFORE SIGNING TO **CARDIFF CITY** IN 2006, GOING ON TO PLAY FOR **CELTIC**, **DUNDEE UNITED**, **MIDDLESBROUGH**, **ABERDEEN** AND MORE?

**4** WHICH **SCOTLAND** INTERNATIONAL SPENT NINE YEARS AT **COVENTRY CITY**, SCORED FOR **CITY** IN THE 1981 FA CUP FINAL AND PLAYED FOR A NUMBER OF CLUBS WELL INTO HIS FORTIES.

**5** WHICH **CITY** MANAGER ALSO TOOK CHARGE OF **COVENTRY CITY**, **SUNDERLAND**, **LEEDS UNITED**, **PLYMOUTH ARGYLE** AND **THAILAND'S** NATIONAL TEAM?

**6** NAME THE **ENGLAND** WINGER WHOSE LENGTHY LIST OF CLUBS INCLUDES **MANCHESTER CITY**, **MANCHESTER UNITED**, **LEEDS UNITED** AND **COVENTRY CITY**.

**7** WHICH **CITY** MANAGER PLAYED FOR **CITY**, **COVENTRY CITY**, **NOTTINGHAM FOREST** AND A NUMBER OF OTHER CLUBS?

**8** NAME **SCOTLAND'S** 1998 WORLD CUP CAPTAIN WHO PLAYED FOR **BLACKBURN ROVERS**, **MANCHESTER CITY**, **RANGERS**, **COVENTRY CITY**, **BOLTON WANDERERS** AND **BLACKPOOL**.

**9** CAPPED 62 TIMES BY *WALES*, WHICH MIDFIELDER PLAYED FOR *PLYMOUTH ARGYLE, MANCHESTER CITY, COVENTRY CITY, NORWICH CITY, NOTTINGHAM FOREST, HUDDERSFIELD TOWN, LINCOLN CITY* AND *STEVENAGE BOROUGH* IN HIS 20-YEAR CAREER?

**10** WHICH *BOLTON WANDERERS, COVENTRY CITY* AND *CARDIFF CITY* MANAGER WOULD SUBSEQUENTLY SERVE AS ASSISTANT MANAGER AND THEN CARETAKER MANAGER OF *CITY* IN THE 1990S?

# "MIGHTY MOUSE"

A TWO-TIME WINNER OF THE BALLON D'OR, **KEVIN KEEGAN** HAD A STELLAR CAREER AS A PLAYER WITH **SCUNTHORPE UNITED,** **LIVERPOOL, HAMBURGER SV** -- WHERE HE EARNED HIS "MIGHTY MOUSE" NICKNAME -- **SOUTHAMPTON** AND **NEWCASTLE UNITED,** BEFORE EMBARKING ON HIS MANAGEMENT CAREER.

SPOT THE **CITY** MANAGER BY THE CLUBS THEY PLAYED FOR:

**1** *CROOK TOWN, NEWCASTLE UNITED, NOTTINGHAM FOREST*

**2** *MANCHESTER UNITED, BARCELONA, BAYERN MUNICH, CHELSEA, SOUTHAMPTON, EVERTON, BLACKBURN ROVERS*

**3** *BOLTON WANDERERS, EVERTON, QUEENS PARK RANGERS, MANCHESTER CITY, SOUTHAMPTON, NOTTS COUNTY, BURY*

**4** *BARCELONA, BRESCIA, ROMA, AL-AHLI, DORADOS*

**5** *TRANMERE ROVERS, MANCHESTER UNITED*

**6** *HEDNESFORD TOWN, PORT VALE, BRIGHTON & HOVE ALBION, LUTON TOWN, HULL CITY.*

**7** *BOLOGNA, SAMPDORIA, LAZIO, LEICESTER CITY*

**8** *WEALDSTONE, COVENTRY CITY, NOTTINGHAM FOREST, NEWCASTLE UNITED, WEST HAM UNITED, MANCHESTER CITY*

**9** *PRESTON NORTH END, EVERTON, BIRMINGHAM CITY, STOKE CITY, BLACKBURN ROVERS*

**10** *EVERTON, MANCHESTER CITY, BRISTOL CITY, NORWICH CITY*

**11** *WEST HAM UNITED, TORQUAY UNITED*

**12** *ASHTON UNITED, BLACKPOOL, EVERTON, ARSENAL, HELLENIC, SOUTHAMPTON, PHILADELPHIA FURY, VANCOUVER WHITECAPS, FLOREAT ATHENA, EASTERN AA, BRISTOL ROVERS*

# NELLIE'S LEFT FOOT

BORN AND RAISED WITHIN A FEW HUNDRED YARDS OF *MAINE ROAD*, *NEIL YOUNG* LIVED THE BOYHOOD DREAM, HIS GOALS PROPELLING *CITY* TO LEAGUE AND EUROPEAN GLORY AND SCORING THE WINNING GOAL IN AN FA CUP FINAL. THE 1970 DEATH OF A BROTHER AFFECTED HIM DEEPLY AND HIS FORM SUFFERED DRAMATICALLY. *"NELLIE"* DRIFTED DOWN THE DIVISIONS AND ENDURED ILLNESS AND FINANCIAL DIFFICULTIES IN LATER YEARS. HE DIED IN EARLY 2011, TWO WEEKS BEFORE HIS 67TH BIRTHDAY.

**1** WHO WAS THE *CITY* MANAGER WHO GAVE THE 17-YEAR-OLD HIS SENIOR DEBUT IN NOVEMBER, 1961?

**2** *YOUNG* SCORED TWICE IN THE 4-3 VICTORY AT *NEWCASTLE UNITED* ON THE LAST DAY OF THE SEASON IN 1968 WHICH SEALED *CITY'S* FIRST LEAGUE TITLE IN 21 YEARS - WHO SCORED *CITY'S* OTHER TWO GOALS THAT DAY?

**3** HE SCORED THE ONLY GOAL OF THE GAME IN THE 1969 CUP FINAL, HITTING THE WINNER PAST WHICH *LEICESTER CITY* GOALKEEPER?

**4** *NEIL* SCORED ONE OF THE GOALS IN *CITY'S* 2-1 VICTORY OVER POLAND'S *GÓRNIK ZABRZE* IN THE 1970 EUROPEAN CUP WINNERS' CUP FINAL -- IN WHICH CITY AND COUNTRY WAS THAT FINAL HELD?

**5** *NEIL* JOINED *PRESTON NORTH END* IN 1972. WHICH TEAMMATE OF *NEIL'S* IN THE SIDES THAT WON THE FA CUP AND EUROPEAN CUP WINNERS' CUP WOULD LATER PLAY FOR AND MANAGE *PRESTON?*

**6** *NEIL* FINISHED HIS CAREER AT WHICH LANCASHIRE CLUB?

**7** WHAT WAS THE TITLE OF *NEIL'S* 2004 AUTOBIOGRAPHY?

# SPLASH THE CASH!

THE 2011 ACQUISITION OF **SERGIO AGÜERO** FROM **ATLÉTICO MADRID** FOR A REPORTED FEE OF £35 MILLION REPRESENTS ONE OF THE BEST INVESTMENTS IN **MANCHESTER CITY** HISTORY.

WHO WERE THE SUBJECTS OF THESE TRANSFERS?

**1** £10,000, FEBRUARY 1936, FROM **BLACKPOOL**

**2** £25,000, JULY 1950, FROM **SWANSEA TOWN**

**3** £55,000, MARCH 1960, FROM **HUDDERSFIELD TOWN**

**4** £60,000, OCTOBER 1967, FROM **BOLTON WANDERERS**

**5** £200,000, MARCH 1972, FROM **QUEENS PARK RANGERS**

**6** £275,000, MARCH 1974, FROM **SUNDERLAND**

**7** £1,437,500, SEPTEMBER 1979, FROM **WOLVERHAMPTON WANDERERS**

**8** £5,000,000, FEBRUARY 2002, FROM **PRESTON NORTH END**

**9** £13,000,000, JUNE 2002, FROM **PARIS SAINT-GERMAIN**

**10** £32,500,000, SEPTEMBER 2008, FROM **REAL MADRID**

**11** £62,600,000, JULY 2019, FROM **ATLÉTICO MADRID**

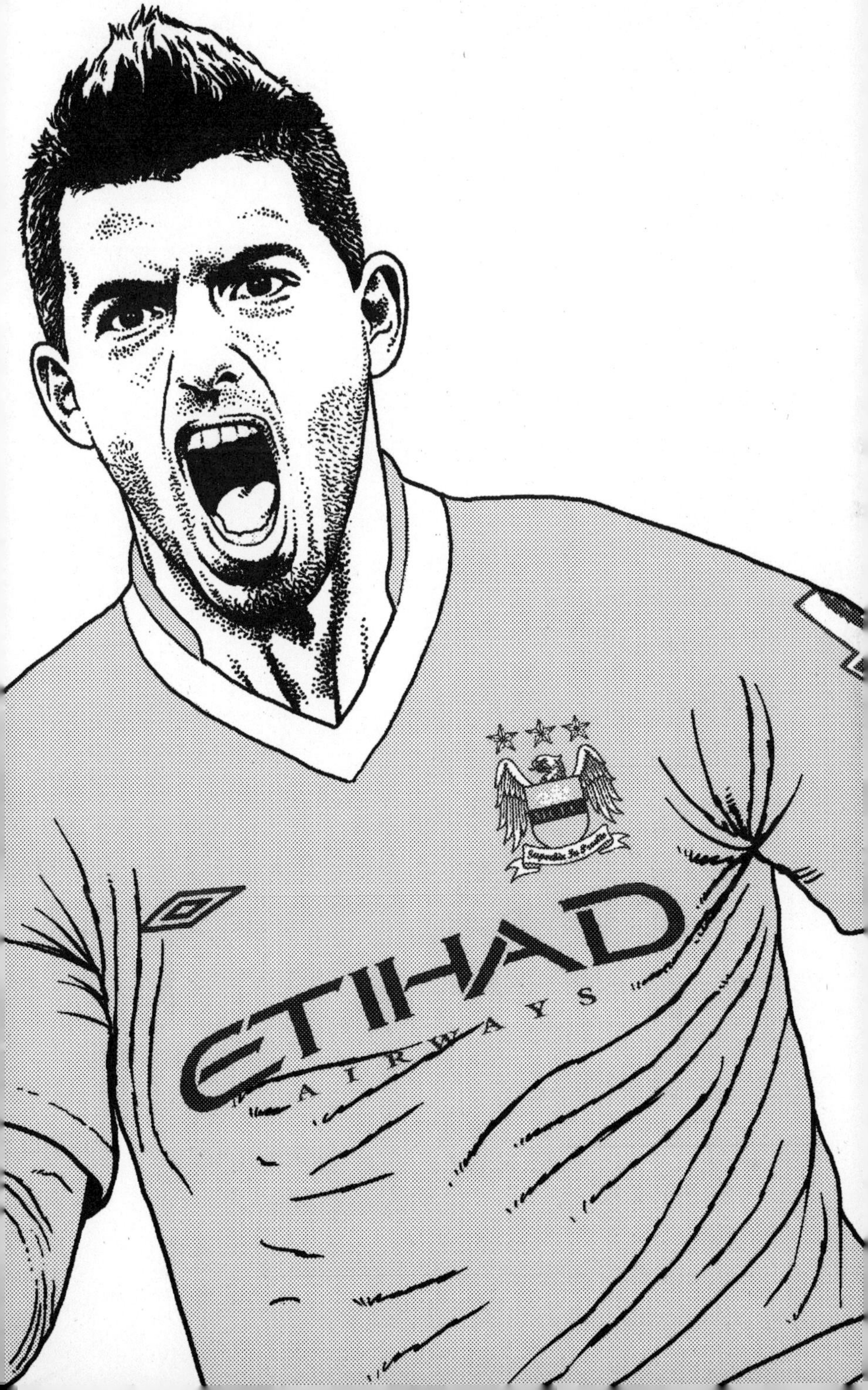
ETIHAD
AIRWAYS

# 1001 ANSWERS

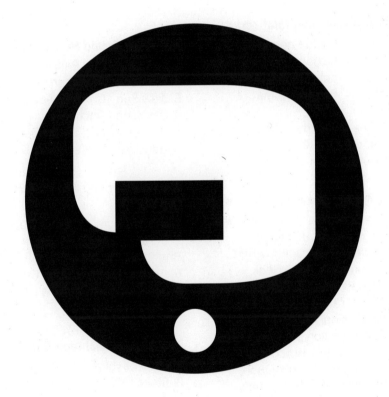

## "The Welsh Wizard" (pg 2)

1. Bolton Wanderers   2. c) Crystal Palace   3. c) Chew a toothpick
4. Manchester United   5. Hyde Road   6. Glyn Pardoe   7. Sergio Aguero, Eric Brook, Tommy Johnson, Colin Bell   8. British Home Championship   9. Roy Paul
10. Mark Hughes

## "We've Got Guardiola" (pg 4)

1. Six   2. Ronald Koeman
3. Bobby Robson, Louis van Gaal, Carles Rexach, Lorenzo Serra Ferrer   4. Brescia, Roma
5. Qatar   6. 1992
7. Frank Rijkaard   8. Two
9. Jupp Heynckes
10. Dorados del Sinaloa

## The Mighty Oakes (pg 6)

1. Joe Corrigan   2. Les McDowall, George Poyser, Joe Mercer, Malcolm Allison, Johnny Hart, Ron Saunders, Tony Book
3. Glyn Pardoe   4. European Cup Winners' Cup, Football League First Division, Football League Second Division, FA Cup, League Cup   5. Tommy Hutchison
6. Aston Villa, Scarborough, Wolverhampton Wanderers, Cardiff City   7. West Bromwich Albion, Aston Villa   8. Chester City   9. Northwich Victoria
10. Port Vale

## "Viva Espana" (pg 8)

1. Jesús Navas   2. Javi García
3. Javier Garrido   4. Alvaro Negredo   5. Ferran Torres

6. Angeliño   7. Aymeric Laporte
8. Rodri   9. Eric García
10. Brahim Díaz

## Off to the Toffees! (pg 10)

1. Paul Power   2. Fabian Delph
3. Brian Kidd   4. Andy Hinchcliffe
5. Sylvain Distin   6. Carlo Nash
7. Alan Harper   8. Terry Phelan
9. Mark Ward   10. Gareth Barry

## Not From Round Here (pg 12)

1. Switzerland   2. Benjani
3. Bermuda   4. Vedran Corluka
5. Jihai Sun   6. Martin Petrov
7. Oleksandr Zinchenko
8. Stevan Jovetic, Stefan Savic
9. Romania   10. Kazimierz Deyna

## The Plumber and The Potters (pg 14)

1. Wilfried Bony   2. Peter Dobing
3. Stephen Ireland   4. Ian Brightwell   5. John Gidman
6. Adrian Heath   7. John Guidetti
8. Joe Corrigan   9. Mike Doyle
10. Paul Stewart

## The Bosnian Diamond (pg 16)

1. VfL Wolfsburg   2. Robinho
3. Stoke City   4. Tottenham Hotspur   5. Pablo Zabaleta
6. Sunderland   7. Roma
8. Aleksandar Kolarov   9. Claudio Ranieri   10. Iran

## The Honorary President (pg 18)

1. Bath City   2. Toronto
3. Plymouth Argyle   4. Johnny Crossan   5. Dave Mackay

6. Johnny Hart   7. Ron Saunders
8. 1976 League Cup
9. Huddersfield Town
10. Peter Reid

## "El Apache" Tevez (pg 20)

1. Boca Juniors   2. Corinthians
3. Zico, Elías Figueroa
4. Paraguay   5. Javier
Mascherano   6. Chelsea
7. Dimitar Berbatov   8. Bayern
Munich   9. Juventus
10. Shanghai Shenhua

## "Life is So Good in America ..." (pg 22)

1. Columbus Crew   2. Kevin
Bond   3. Alan Ball   4. San Diego
Sockers   5. Bradley Wright-
Phillips   6. Jack Harrison
7. David Johnson   8. Brian Kidd
9. Adrian Heath   10. Patrick Vieira

## Australian, Thai and Indian Takeaways (pg 24)

1. Steve McMahon   2. Danny
Tiatto   3. Aaron Mooy   4. Niall
Quinn   5. Sven-Göran Eriksson
6. Thaksin Shinawatra   7. David
James   8. Nicolas Anelka
9. Steve Coppell   10. Terry Phelan

## The Boys From Brazil (pg 26)

1. Shakhtar Donetsk
2. Internazionale   3. CSKA
Moscow   4. Porto   5. Vasco
da Gama   6. Palmeiras   7. Real
Madrid   8. Barcelona   9. Benfica
10. 1. FC Nürnberg

## The Centurions (pg 28)

1. Shay Given   2. Roque Santa
Cruz   3. Robinho   4. Peter
Schmeichel   5. Vedran Ćorluka
6. frank Lampard   7. Claudio
Bravo   8. Kolo Touré   9. Yaya
Touré   10. David Silva

## Ten Tykes (pg 30)

1. Kieran Trippier   2. Gerry
Taggart   3. Devante Cole
4. John Stones   5. Joe Hayes
6. Lee Crooks   7. Alan Ogley
8. John Beresford   9. Jon Macken
10. Mick McCarthy

## "Maverick" Marsh (pg 32)

1. Fulham   2. West Bromwich
Albion   3. Malcolm Allison
4. Wolverhampton Wanderers
5. Johnny Hart, Ron Saunders,
Tony Book   6. Tampa Bay
Rowdies   7. George Best
8. Alec Stock   9. New York
United, Carolina Lightnin',
Tampa Bay Rowdies
10. Bradford City

## City POTY (pg 34)

1. Asa Hartford, Neil McNab
(twice), Colin Hendry   2. Mick
McCarthy, Niall Quinn, Richard
Dunne (four), Stephen Ireland
3. Ali Benarbia   4. Tony Coton
5. Gerard Wiekens   6. Sergio
Agüero   7. Uwe Rösler
8. Kevin De Bruyne ( three to
date)   9. Sylvain Distin
10. Dave Watson

### "It's Hammer Time!" (pg 36)

1. Joe Hart   2. Justin Fashanu
3. Trevor Morley   4. Wayne
Bridge   5. Kevin Horlock   6. Ian
Bishop   7. Steve Lomas   8. Craig
Bellamy   9. Trevor Sinclair
10. David Cross

### Big Mal (pg 38)

1. West Ham United
2. Tuberculosis   3. Bath City,
Toronto City, Plymouth Argyle
4. Crystal Palace   5. Galatasaray
6. Peter Swales   7. Steve Daley
8. John Bond   9. Sporting CP
10. Kuwait

### Roque of the Rovers (pg 40)

1. Garry Flitcroft   2. Peter Dobing
3. Tosin Adarabioyo   4. Colin
Hendry   5. Nicky Reid   6. Gunnar
Nielsen   7. Benjani   8. Craig
Bellamy   9. Andy Cole
10. Paul Dickov

### "Niall Quinn's Disco Pants Are The Best" (pg 42)

1. Arsenal   2. Howard Kendall
3. Peter Reid, Tony Book
(caretaker), Brian Horton, Alan
Ball   4. Tony Coton   5. Kevin
Phillips   6. Frank Stapleton
7. Robbie Keane   8. 1990 and
2002   9. Peter Reid
10. Ellis Short

### Togo's Go-To Guy (pg 44)

1. Monaco   2. 25   3. Mark Hughes
4. 4-2   5. Robin van Persie
6. Lech Pozna   7. José Mourinho
8. Tottenham Hotspur, Crystal
Palace   9. Turkey, Paraguay
10. 2006

### The Bhoys are Back in Town (pg 46)

1. Kolo Touré   2. Dedrick Boyata
3. Eyal Berkovic   4. Neil Lennon
5. Shay Given   6. John Guidetti
7. Craig Bellamy   8. Jason
Denayer   9. Scott Sinclair
10. Mick McCarthy

### The Happy Wanderers (pg 48)

1. Martin Petrov   2. Vladimír
Weiss   3. Wyn Davies   4. Peter
Beardsley   5. Francis Lee
6. Dedryck Boyata   7. Nicky
Summerbee   8. Jamie Pollock
9. Neil McNab   10. Brian Kidd

### Captain Kid (pg 50)

1. Blue Star   2. Tony Book
3. Huddersfield Town   4. Paul
Stewart, Tony Adcock, David
White   5. Eric Nixon   6. David
Oldfield (2), Trevor Morley, Ian
Bishop, Andy Hinchcliffe
7. Kenny Clements   8. Oldham
Athletic   9. Billy McNeill, Jimmy
Frizzell, Tony Book, Mel Machin,
Howard Kendall, Peter Reid
10. Bury

### Big Meeks (pg 52)

1. Aston Villa   2. Swine Flu
3. Rio Ferdinand   4. Steve
McLaren   5. Fabio Capello
6. Stuart Pearce   7. Craig Bellamy
and Ryan Giggs   8. Fiorentina

9. Aston Villa   10. Roy Keane

## City's Celebs (pg 54)

1. Eddie Large   2. Kevin Cummins
3. Kevin Kennedy   4. Marc Riley
5. Ricky Hatton   6. Andy Connell
7. Timothy Dalton   8. Billy Duffy
9. Alan Rickman   10. Rob Gretton

## The Stockport Iniesta (pg 56)

1. Spain   2. Kelechi Iheanacho
3. Chelsea   4. Arsenal
5. Oxford United   6. Micah
Richards and Daniel Sturridge
7. The 2021 UEFA Champions
League Final   8. Mason
Greenwood   9. Iceland   10. Peter
Barnes, Leroy Sané and Raheem
Sterling while playing for City,
Paul Walsh, Andy Cole, Robbie
Fowler, Nicolas Anelka, Craig
Bellamy and James Milner while
playing for other clubs.

## Catalan Connections (pg 58)

1. Yaya Touré   2. Sergio Agüero
3. Denis Suárez   4. Mark Hughes
5. Txiki Begiristain   6. Nolito
7. Sylvinho   8. Ferran Soriano
9. Mikel Arteta   10. New York

## Molineux-bies (pg 60)

1. Jimmy Murray   2. Bobby
McDonald   3. Dave Wagstaffe
4. Eric Nixon   5. Steve Daley
6. Paul Simpson   7. Paul Stewart
8. Barry Stobart   9. John
Burridge   10. Joleon Lescott

## Bled Blue Blood (pg 62)

1. Tommy   2. Harry Godwin
3. Tony Book   4. Carlos Tevez, FA
Cup, 2011   5. a) Five   6. Rodney
Marsh   7. Stoke City   8. Bolton
Wanderers   9. Rochdale
10. Glyn Pardoe

## Crème de la Prem (pg 64)

1. John Burridge   2. Andy Cole
3. 134   4. Richard Dunne
5. Alan Shearer, Andy Cole,
Jermain Defoe, Dimitar Berbatov
6. Thierry Henry   7. Richard
Dunne, Patrick Vieira   8. Joe Hart
9. Five   10. Craig Bellamy,
seven teams

## Thrashings! (pg 66)

1. Lincoln City   2. Small Heath
3. Watford   4. Middlesbrough
5. Liverpool Stanley   6. Bradford
Park Avenue   7. Burton Albion
8. Liverpool   9. Schalke 04
10. Barcelona

## "Uncle Joe" Mercer (pg 68)

1. Everton   2. Arsenal
3. Sheffield United, Aston Villa
4. George Poyser   5. Albert
Alexander   6. Coventry City
7. Tony Coleman, Ian Bowyer
8. Alf Ramsey   9. Eamonn
Andrews   10. Peter Doherty

## "The Honey Monster" (pg 70)

1. Joe Royle   2. Laurent Charvet
3. Garry Cook   4. Aston Villa
5. Martin O'Neill   6. Manchester
United   7. Queens Park Rangers

8. Kevin Bond   9. Mick McCarthy
10. Martin O'Neill

### The Derby (pg 72)
1. Johnny Evans   2. George
Best   3. Mike Doyle   4. Alf-Inge
Haaland   5. Marouane Fellaini
6. Colin Bell   7. Cristiano Ronaldo
8. Gary Neville   9. Brian Kidd
10. Vincent Kompany

### A Man in a Million (pg 74)
1. John Bond   2. Czechoslovakia
and Kuwait   3. Jimmy Hill
4. Sampdoria   5. Atalanta
6. Rangers   7. Queens Park
Rangers   8. Sheffield Wednesday
9. Birmingham City
10. Crystal Palace

### Buzzer! (pg 76)
1. Neil Young (2) and Francis Lee
2. George Best   3. Asa Hartford
4. Burnley   5. Blackpool
6. Stockport County   7. Sid
Harmor   8. Nicky Summerbee
9. b) Eight   10. Club Ambassador

### Travelling The East Lancs Road (pg 78)
1. Steve McManaman   2. Nigel
Clough   3.Scott Carson   4. Paul
Walsh   5. Kolo Touré   6. Steve
McMahon   7. Sir Matt Busby
8. Peter Beardsley   9. Paul
Stewart   10. David Johnson.

### Going For Gold (pg 80)
1. Kazimierz Deyna   2. Poland
3. David Pizarro   4. Carlos Tevez

5. Sergio Agüero   6. Pablo
Zabaleta   7. Jô

### Going Up! (pg 82)
1. Sam Omerod   2. Sam Omerod
3. Tom Maley   4. Harry Newbould
5. Peter Hodge   6. Sam Cowan
7. Les McDowall   8. Joe Mercer
9. Billy McNeill   10. Mel Machin
11. Kevin Keegan

### City's Africans (pg 84)
1. Algeria   2. Ivory Coast
3. Cameroon   4. Liberia   5. Ivory
Coast   6. Nigeria   7. Togo
8. Algeria   9. Zimbabwe
10. Liberia

### "Bobby Manc" (pg 86)
1. Sampdoria   2. Carlos Tevez
3. Lazio   4. Leicester City
5. a) 36   6. Internazionale
7. Mark Hughes   8. Galatasaray
9. Zenit Saint Petersburg
10. Gian Piero Ventura

### The Scandinavians  (pg 88)
1. Danish   2. Danish
3. Norwegian   4. Danish
5. Swedish   6. Danish
7. Norwegian   8. Danish
9. Norwegian   10. Norwegian

### Them's The Breaks (pg 90)
1. Harry Dowd   2. Vincent
Kompany   3. Álvaro Negredo
4. Aymeric Laporte   5. Gabriel
Jesus   6. Kevin De Bruyne
7. Mike Summerbee
8. Bill Leivers

### You Know My Name (pg 92)

1. 21   2. Marc-Vivien Foé
3. Emmanuel Adebayor   4. Edin Džeko   5. 5   6. The 1933 FA Cup Final – Everton wore numbers 1 through 11 and neither team was allowed to wear their customary blue shirts   7. 18

### Boss Men (pg 94)

1. Joe Royle   2. Martin O'Neill
3. Peter Reid   4. Les McDowall
5. Don Revie   6. Tony Book
7. Neil Lennon   8. Steve McMahon
9. Mick McCarthy   10. Keith Curle

### Back of the Net! (pg 96)

1. Billy Meredith   2. Fred Tilson (2)   3. Joe Hayes, Jack Dyson, Bobby Johnstone   4. Neil Young
5. Mike Doyle, Glyn Pardoe
6. Neil Young, Francis Lee
7. Yaya Touré   8. Yaya Touré, Samir Nasri, Jesús Navas
9. Fernandinho (Penalties: Jesús Navas, Sergio Agüero, Yaya Touré)   10. Sergio Agüero, Vincent Kompany, David Silva
11. (Penalties: İlkay Gündoğan, Sergio Agüero, Bernardo Silva, Raheem Sterling)   12. Gabriel Jesus (2), Raheem Sterling (2), David Silva, Kevin De Bruyne
13. Sergio Agüero, Rodri
14. Aymeric Laporte

### The Notorious KDB (p98)

1. Genk   2. André Villas-Boas and Roberto Di Matteo   3. Werder Bremen   4. Wolfsburg
5. Jérôme Boateng   6. Manuel Pellegrini   7. Thierry Henry
8. Mark Hughes   9. Georges Leekens, Marc Wilmots, Roberto Martinez   10. Antonio Rüdiger

### The Boys in Green (pg 100)

1. Mick McCarthy   2. Niall Quinn
3. Stephen Ireland   4. Michael Robinson   5. Ron Healey   6. Jon Macken   7. Eddie McGoldrick
8. Terry Phelan   9. Richard Dunne
10. Jimmy Conway

### Back Room Boys (pg 102)

1. Brian Kidd   2. Mikel Arteta
3. Stuart Pearce   4. Phil Neal
5. Ken Barnes   6. Eddie Niedzwiecki   7. Willie Donachie
8. Asa Hartford   9. Jimmy Frizzell
10. Patrick Vieira

### The Paratrooper (pg 104)

1. b) Bremen   2. St. Helens
3. Jock Thomson   4. Don Revie
5. Telford United   6. Stockport County   7. Burma (now Myanmar)   8. Tanzania, Liberia, Pakistan and North Yemen
9. Spain   10. "The Keeper"

### Bonded to Bond (pg 106)

1. Gerry Gow   2. Martin O'Neill
3. Age Hareide   4. David Cross
5. Chris Jones   6. Phil Boyer
7. Kevin Bond   8. Trevor Francis
9. John Ryan   10. Tommy Hutchison

### Sterling Stuff (pg 108)

1. d) Jamaica   2. Shaquille O'Neal

3. Queens Park Rangers
4. Rafael Benítez   5. Antonio
Valencia   6. Wayne Rooney
7. John Stones   8. Bournemouth
9. Czech Republic   10. Mike Dean

## 2006 World Cup (pg 110)

1. Patrick Vieira   2. Corinthians
3. City's David James plus Scott
Carson, Wayne Bridge, Owen
Hargreaves and Frank Lampard
4. Olimpiacos   5. Roque Santa
Cruz   6. Ajax   7. DaMarcus
Beasley   8. Togo
9. Real Madrid   10. Sven-Göran
Eriksson (England)

## The Goal Machine (pg 112)

1. Independiente   2. Diego
Maradona   3. Atlético Madrid
4. Nigeria   5. Swansea City   6. 16
7. Eric Brook   8. Wayne Rooney
9. Lionel Messi, Gabriel Batistuta
10. Benjamin

## World Cup Bosses (pg 114)

1. Alan Ball   2. Colin Bell and
Francis Lee   3. Asa Hartford
(Scotland)   4. Steve Coppell, Phil
Neal (England) and Asa Hartford
(Scotland)   5. Peter Reid
6. Roberto Mancini (Italy)
7. Stuart Pearce, Peter Beardsley,
David Seaman, Steve McMahon
8. Phil Neal   9. Pep Guardiola

## "Allez Les Bleus!" (pg 116)

1. Monaco   2. Porto
3. Arsenal   4. Lazio   5. Lens
6. Internazionale   7. Paris Saint-
Germain   8. Arsenal
9. Newcastle United
10. Paris Saint-Germain

## Campeones (pg 118)

1. a) Benfica  b) Monaco
2. Benfica   3. a) Benfica
b) Juventus   4. Leicester City
5. Monaco   6. Shakhtar Donetsk
7. Genk   8. Palmeiras
9. Borussia Dortmund
10. Queens Park Rangers

## The Ones That Got Away (pg 120)

1. Ryan Giggs   2. Adrien Rabiot
3. Eric Garcia   4. Kieran Trippier
5. Ben Mee   6. Brahim Díaz
7. John Guidetti   8. John
Sheridan   9. Denis Suárez
10. Jason Denayer

## "Safe Hands" Seaman (pg 122)

1. Leeds United   2. Peterborough
3. Ron Saunders   4. Jim Smith
5. Bobby Robson   6. George
Graham   7. Parma   8. Kevin
Keegan   9. "They Think It's All
Over"   10. b) 75

## Captains Fantastic (pg 124)

1. Billy Meredith   2. Sam Cowan
3. Roy Paul   4. Tony Book
5. Tony Book   6. Tony Book
7. Mike Doyle   8. Carlos Tevez
9. David Silva   10. Fernandinho

## The Lawman (pg 126)

1. Huddersfield Town   2. Bill
Shankly   3. Les McDowall

4. Torino   5. Matt Busby
6. Johnny Hart   7. Kenny Dalglish
8. Peter Doherty   9. 1974
10. Aberdeen

### In Search of a Title (pg 128)

1. James Milner   2. Francis Lee
3. Billy Meredith   4. Ian Bowyer
5. Colin Hendry   6. Michael
Robinson   7. Daniel Sturridge
8. Kasper Schmeichel   9. Tommy
Johnson   10. Nicolas Anelka

### Golden Gloves Hart (pg 130)

1. Shrewsbury Town
2. Tranmere Rovers and Blackpool
3. Andreas Isaksson   4. Shay
Given   5. Birmingham City
6. Torino   7. West Ham United
8. Burnley   9. Tottenham Hotspur
10. Petr Čech

### A Red-Headed Genius (pg 132)

1. Sammy McIlroy   2. Martin
O'Neill   3. Johnny Crossan
4. Kevin Horlock   5. Steve Lomas
6. Neil Lennon

### City and the San Siro (pg 134)

1. Santos   2. Mario Balotelli
3. Maicon   4. Brian Kidd
5. Patrick Vieira   6. Nigel De Jong
7. Roberto Mancini   8. Herbert
Burgess   9. George Weah
10. Stevan Jovetić

### Chelsea Connections (pg 136)

1. Wayne Bridge   2. Shaun
Wright-Phillips   3. Derek Kevan
4. Tal Ben Haim   5. David

Rocastle   6. Colin Viljoen
7. Willy Caballero   8. Clive Allen
9. Gordon Davies
10. Clive Wilson

### King of The Kippax (pg 138)

1. Bury   2. Nijinsky   3. 1965–66
Football League Second Division,
1967–68 Football League First
Division, 1968–69 FA Cup, 1969–
70 Football League Cup, 1969–70
European Cup Winners' Cup
4. Alf Ramsey, Joe Mercer, Don
Revie   5. Romania
6. Manchester United   7. Joe
Mercer, Malcolm Allison, Johnny
Hart, Tony Book, Ron Saunders
8. San Jose Earthquakes
9. "Reluctant Hero"   10. MBE

### "Oor Wullie" (pg 140)

1. First Division champions Derby
County and FA Cup holders
Leeds United declined to play
and so City, who had finished
fourth, and Third Division
champions Villa were invited
to contest the game.   2. Glyn
Pardoe   3. Portland Timbers
4. Norwich City   5. Burnley
6. Oldham Athletic
7. Manchester United   8. Ipswich
Town   9. Millwall   10. Montserrat

### Hartford's Heart (pg 142)

1. West Bromwich Albion
2. Malcolm Allison
3. Nottingham Forest   4. John
Benson   5. Sunderland   6. Phil
Neal   7. Stockport County
8. Stoke City   9. Alan Ball

10. Macclesfield Town

### The Boys of 2012 (pg 144)

1. Fiorentina on loan then Aston Villa   2. West Bromwich Albion
3. Roma   4. Fiorentina
5. İstanbul Başakşehir
6. Sunderland   7. Everton
8. Liverpool   9. AC Milan
10. Juventus

### 2014 World Cup (pg 146)

1. Wilfried Bony   2. Fernandinho, Maicon and Jô   3. Jérôme Boateng   4. Gelson Fernandes
5. Vincent Kompany, Daniel Van Buyten, Kevin De Bruyne
6. Pablo Zabaleta, Martín Demichelis, Sergio Agüero
7. Ecuador   8. Georgios Samaras
9. Joe Hart, James Milner, Daniel Sturridge, Raheem Sterling, Frank Lampard   10. DaMarcus Beasley

### Franny Lee (pg 148)

1. Bolton Wanderers   2. Neil Young   3. Wayne Rooney
4. Peter Kay   5. Brazil   6. Dave Mackay   7. Norman Hunter
8. Peter Swales   9. Alan Ball, Asa Hartford, Steve Coppell, Phil Neal, Frank Clark   10. Denis Law

### Proud Peacocks (pg 150)

1. Fabian Delph   2. Darren Huckerby   3. Danny Mills
4. Don Revie   5. David White
6. Richard Jobson   7. Derek Parlane   8. Alf-Inge Haaland
9. Bobby McDonald

10. Peter Barnes

### City's Dragons (pg 152)

1. Roy Paul   2. Kit Symons
3. Wyn Davies   4. Mark Hughes
5. Roy Clarke   6. Gordon Davies
7. Billy Meredith   8. Cliff Sear

### Danger Men At Work (pg 154)

1. David James   2. Tony Coton
3. Andy Dibble   4. Harry Dowd
5. Ederson   6. Claudio Bravo
7. Richard Wright   8. Joe Corrigan   9. Joe Hart

### Madridistas y Colchoneros (pg 156)

1. Tottenham Hotspur   2. 16
3. Martín Demichelis   4. Steve McManaman   5. Kiki Musampa
6. Gabriel Jesus   7. Danilo
8. Rodri   9. Manuel Pellegrini
10. Martin Petrov

### Monaco Men (pg 158)

1. Benjamin Mendy   2. Maicon
3. Ali Benarbia   4. Emmanuel Adebayor   5. Ousmane Dabo
6. George Weah   7. Bernardo Silva   8. Rony Lopes

### The "Nutter With The Putter" Affair! (pg 160)

1. Norwich City   2. Coventry City
3. Newcastle United   4. Celtic
5. Blackburn Rovers   6. Liverpool
7. West Ham United
8. Manchester City
9. Cardiff City

### Between The Sticks (pg 162)

1. Kyle Walker   2. Tony Coton
3. David James   4. Eike Immel
5. Gunnar Nielsen   6. Costel
Pantilimon   7. John Burridge
8. First goalkeeper in history
to score from open play with a
clearance   9. Bobby McDonald
10. Tommy Wright

### 2018 World Cup (pg 164)

1. Dedryck Boyata   2. John
Stones   3. Aaron Mooy
4. Aleksandar Kolarov   5. Kevin
De Bruyne and a Fernandinho
own goal, both for Belgium
6. Willy Caballero   7. Kasper
Schmeichel   8. Nigeria
9. Benjamin Mendy
10. Åge Hareide

### Arsenal Connections (pg 166)

1. Dave Bacuzzi   2. David Seaman
3. Bacary Sagna   4. Brian Kidd
5. Eddie McGoldrick   6. Paul
Dickov   7. Gaël Clichy

### "Bravehearts" (pg 168)

1. Denis Law   2. Matt Busby
3. Paul Dickov   4. Asa Hartford
5. Jimmy McMullan
6. Ralph Brand

### Portuguese Men o' City (pg 170)

1. Porto and Benfica   2. Benfica
3. Benfica   4. Sporting CP
5. Porto   6. Porto and Estrela da
Amadora   7. Benfica
8. Benfica   9. Porto

### Psycho! (pg 172)

1. Wealdstone   2. Coventry City
3. Frank Clark   4. Newcastle
United   5. Harry Redknapp
6. Sven-Göran Eriksson
7. Fabio Capello

### So Long (pg 174)

1. Galatasaray   2. Saint-Étienne
3. Portsmouth   4. Ankaragücü
5. Parma (loan)   6. Notts County
7. Aston Villa   8. Sheffield United
9. Birmingham City (loan)
10. Cardiff City (loan)

### Roberto's Recruits (pg 176)

1. Everton   2. Benfica   3. Partizan
4. Internazionale   5. Fiorentina
6. Manchester United   7. Lazio
8. Preston North End   9. Swansea
City   10. Hamburger SV   11. Aston
Villa   12. Internazionale

### Euro 2020 Vision (pg 178)

1. Wayne Hennessey, David
Brooks, Matthew Smith
2. João Cancelo   3. Ferran Torres,
Aymeric Laporte, Rodri and Eric
Garcia   4. Jadon Sancho and
Kieran Trippier   5. Two - Ilkay
Gündoğan and Leroy Sané
6. Dedryck Boyata and Jason
Denayer   7. Róbert Mak and
Vladimír Weiss   8. Sweden

### Psycho's Signings! (pg 180)

1. Aston Villa   2. Valencia
3. Shrewsbury Town   4. Bolton
Wanderers   5. Blackburn Rovers
6. Ajax   7. Espanyol

8. Stade Rennais   9. Lazio
10. PSV Eindhoven

## German Exports (pg 182)

1. FC Schalke 04   2. Borussia
Dortmund   3. Hamburger SV
4. Bayern Munich   5. 1.FC
Saarbrücken   6. Borussia
Mönchengladbach   7. VfB
Stuttgart   8. Eintracht Frankfurt
9. Borussia Dortmund
10. 1.FC Nürnberg

## The "Revie Plan" Man (pg 184)

1. David Watson   2. Mick Channon
3. Colin Bell   4. Dennis Tueart
5. David Johnson   6. Mike Doyle
7. Joe Corrigan   8. Trevor Francis
9. Tony Towers   10. Stan Bowles

## Anarchic Anelka (pg 186)

1. Paris Saint-Germain
2. Newcastle United   3. Real
Madrid   4. El Hadji Diouf
5. Kevin Keegan   6. Fenerbahçe
7. Sam Allardyce, Sammy Lee,
Gary Megson   8. Robin van
Persie   9. Juventus   10. West
Bromwich Albion
11. Mumbai City

## Calamity James (pg 188)

1. Watford   2. Liverpool   3. Aston
Villa   4. West Ham United
5. David Seaman   6. Cardiff City
7. Chelsea   8. Petr Čech   9. Harry
Redknapp, Tony Adams, Paul
Hart, Avram Grant   10. Bristol
City   11. AFC Bournemouth
12. Iceland   13. India

## Make 'em Mackems (pg 190)

1. Jason Denayer   2. Tal Ben Haim
3. Nedum Onuoha   4. Benjani
5. Tony Towers   6. Micky Horswill
7. Don Revie   8. Márton Fülöp
9. Wayne Bridge
10. Jack Rodwell

## The Man With One Name (pg 192)

1. Rodri   2. Angeliño   3. Maicon
4. Nolito   5. Elano   6. Sylvinho
7. Fernando   8. Sylvinho
9. Geovanni   10. Gláuber

## It's A Family Affair (pg 194)

1. Summerbee   2. Paul and Ron
Futcher   3. Alan Oakes
4. Tommy Doyle   5. Yaya and
Kolo Touré   6. Shaun Wright-
Phillips and Bradley Wright-
Phillips   7. Kevin Bond   8. Ian and
David Brightwell   9. Barnes
10. Andy and Devante Cole
11. Nmecha   12. Whitley
13. Roberto Mancini

## Palace Intrigue (pg 196)

1. Roberto Mancini   2. Alan Ball
3. Malcolm Allison   4. Howard
Kendall   5. Sven-Göran Eriksson
6. Mark Hughes   7. Joe Royle
8. Brian Horton   9. Peter Reid

## Sent To Coventry (pg 198)

1. Joe Mercer   2. Kasper
Schmeichel   3. Willo Flood
4. Tommy Hutchison   5. Peter
Reid   6. Peter Barnes   7. Stuart
Pearce   8. Colin Hendry

9. David Phillips 10. Phil Neal

### *"Mighty Mouse" (pg 200)*

1. Frank Clark 2. Mark Hughes
3. Peter Reid 4. Pep Guardiola
5. Steve Coppell 6. Brian Horton
7. Roberto Mancini 8. Stuart
Pearce 9. Howard Kendall
10. Joe Royle 11. John Bond
12. Alan Ball

### *Nellie's Left Foot (pg 202)*

1. Les McDowall 2. Francis Lee
and Mike Summerbee 3. Peter
Shilton 4. Vienna, Austria
5. Tommy Booth 6. Rochdale
7. "Catch a Falling Star"

### *"Splash the Cash" (pg 204)*

1. Peter Doherty 2. Roy Paul
3. Denis Law 4. Francis Lee
5. Rodney Marsh 6. Dennis
Tueart 7. Steve Daley 8. Jon
Macken 9. Nicolas Anelka
10. Robinho 11. Rodri

# TRIVQUIZ

**FROM ABBA TO ZAPPA, AMÉLIE TO ZULU, AND AGÜERO TO ZIDANE**

## NEW FOOTBALL And POP CULTURE QUIZZES
# EVERY DAY AT TRIVQUIZ.COM

 trivquiz.com     trivquiz     trivquiz     trivquizcomic